BODY

SUPREMACY

Exploring the Torment of
Eating Disorders as a Syndrome

ROBIN PHIPPS WOODALL

Dedication

To the miracle and phenomenon that opened my mind to allow me to escape the depths of hell that was securely held captive inside the misery of an eating disorder.

I dedicate this project to the power of courage, humility, and the grace to see things from a more loving point of view.

To the scientists who've devoted thousands of hours exploring the curiosities and intricacies of the human mind and body—not because they want personal gain, but because they are seeking what is important to humanity.

To all of the people who've personally shared their eating disorder experience with me on many levels. They opened up about the truth of their wins and losses, and the vulnerable truth of their struggles. It is their humility and willingness to be honest with me and with themselves that allowed the work I do to evolve.

To the most important people in my life: My mother and father for being the most loving influence in my recovery. And my husband Mark and my children Chloe, Wyatt, and Suzanne—thank you for believing in me, and for having patience during the years I couldn't find the energy, motivation, or discipline to get this work done.

Contents

Introduction   7

SECTION 1

Survival Mode and the Threat of Danger

- Chapter 1:   The Terror Inside an Eating Disorder   23

- Chapter 2:   Evolutionary Psychology and Maslow's
  Lower Hierarchy of Survival Needs   41

- Chapter 3:   The Lower States of Consciousness
  and Survival Mode   59

SECTION 2

Surviving in a Narcissistic Culture

- Chapter 4:   Narcissistic Survival Mode   79

- Chapter 5:   Grandiose Narcissism, Co-Narcissism,
  and Eating Disorders   101

- Chapter 6:   Survival Mode for the Privileged   119

SECTION 3

Killing Yourself to Survive:
Stockholm Syndrome, and Complex PTSD

- Chapter 7:   Trauma Bonding and Stockholm Syndrome   135

- Chapter 8:   Superior Syndrome—When Narcissistic
              Body and Diet Images Combine   155

- Chapter 9:   Trapped Inside Body-Diet Supremacy Syndrome   175

SECTION 4

Accepting Loss, Failure, and Death in Exchange for Freedom

- Chapter 10: Defending the Disorder and Fighting
              to Stay in Captivity   193

- Chapter 11: Leaving Safety and Control
              for the Vulnerability of Freedom   213

- Chapter 12: Hope, Hope, and More Hope   231

Acknowledgments   247

References   249

Introduction

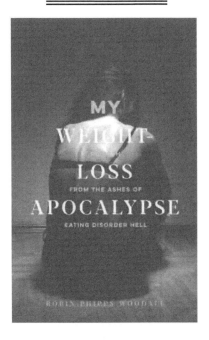

My Weight-Loss Apocalypse

"And once the storm is over, you won't remember how you made it through, how you managed to survive. You won't even be sure, whether the storm is really over. But one thing is certain. When you come out of the storm, you won't be the same person who walked in. That's what this storm's all about."

– Japanese writer, Haruki Murakami

How I Got Here...

It's been over twenty years since I miraculously recovered from the grip of a relentless eating disorder and suicidal depression. In a span of three years, I went from being a cheerful, naive, bright-eyed and energetic freshman in college to being severely depressed, mentally ill, and preparing for suicide before the age of 21.

By the second semester of my sophomore year, my life had spiraled out of control as I tried to cope with depression by losing weight. I quickly lost touch with reality as I suffered with an eating disorder that ultimately changed the course of my life. During that time, I gave up a full-ride scholarship, quit school, married a man I only knew for six months, and moved across the country with him. I was in such a dark, emotional pit of despair that during the first year of being married and within months of moving, I decided to commit suicide. However, during a deep state of contemplation as I emotionally prepared to end my life, I miraculously recovered.

> **NOTE:** What promotes an eating disorder is complex. There isn't one thing that causes an eating disorder but rather, I assume that for me it was a combination of factors that together promoted my need to find something to help me survive. A combination of things in my life supported my inclination toward an eating disorder as a coping mechanism. For me, it was strict patriarchal religious beliefs with rigid standards—and how what happened the first years of college—brought on my need to be in control *of something, when everything in my life seemed to be irreparably damaged.* For whatever reason, I internalized these strict beliefs in such a way that I didn't give myself the forgiveness from my struggles to control my life when objectivity was needed. I couldn't tell the difference between a subjective opinion and reality.

When it comes to other people's stories, and why they might suffer from disordered eating or the severity of an eating disorder, I think it's important to look at it as a collective issue—where separate aspects that come together, and when combined, promote an eating disorder.

Similar to how a "syndrome" is a cluster of symptoms found together, I believe behaviors and thoughts that resemble an eating disorder should be viewed the same way.

Not only did I experience an instantaneous removal from every negative aspect of the disorder and depression, but I also came out of it having a total shift in the way I perceived and lived life.

Afterward, it was discernably clear to me *that the condition of my body was irrelevant as long as it was sufficiently alive to keep me conscious.* The health, leanness, fatness, or attractiveness of my body wasn't important in any way, even if others liked me or disapproved of me because of it. I understood that my body was simply a conduit to experience and express life—and the need to use it to prove myself to others became nonsensical.

I remember afterwards having an intense desire to share my recovery with the world, wanting to shout from the rooftops about the freedom I'd become aware of. But as quickly as I felt the desire to help others, I also felt that my experience might not be meant for others to hear—especially since I didn't quite understand how to explain it. It was a personal experience that felt sacred to me, and I figured that if it were meant to be shared, letting others know about my recovery wouldn't be forced.

There was a sense of peace when I realized that I didn't have to reveal to others what happened, but could peacefully and quietly move on with my life. If the opportunity might arise in the future, then at that point I would share my experience to the best of my ability—but only if it felt appropriate. I didn't tell anyone about my recovery, not even my husband or parents.

They were left to witness my recovery without context for why and how it happened. In my mind, it didn't need to be addressed.

After recovering, I began a new life that I directed from a heart-centered and independent state of mind. The first choice I made was to return to the university I left to earn back my scholarship and finish school. To do this I had to face disappointing many people, as well as live apart from my new husband because we would be attending two different schools across the country from each other. Doing so allowed me the time and space to make decisions for myself, and to develop a sense of autonomy and emotional strength.

I finished college with a bachelor's degree in exercise science, and it made sense to carve out a career as a personal trainer. My husband and I started our family, and I worked in the exercise industry for over thirteen years. Today, I am still married to the same man and we now have three children.

Weight-Loss Apocalypse and the Protocol

Ten years later, in 2007 I was approached to help and monitor people through a medical hormonal therapy that required strict adherence to a very low-calorie protocol. This hormonal therapy was created over decades of observation by Dr. A.T.W Simeons, an endocrinologist who studied the pregnancy hormone: Human Chorionic Gonadotropin (hCG). Dr. Simeons' hCG protocol is very controversial because it lacks scientific credibility. However, when I was approached to assist and monitor people going through the protocol, I was fascinated and curious by the physiology of the process. Because I ran my own gym and owned the necessary equipment, I was able to do a variety of tests to monitor the physical response each patient experienced. Over the course of three years, I felt compelled to publish not only the data I collected regarding the physical results of the medical protocol, but also my observations with respect to the emotional aspects of the protocol as it related to weight loss and emotional eating.

I thoroughly describe the hormonal protocol, give a hypothesis for how it could work, explain my experience working with patients, as well as present the testing results that I gathered in my first book, *Weight-Loss Apocalypse-Book 1* and in my second book, *Weight-Loss Apocalypse Book 2.*

For years, as I met with clients weekly to do testing, I got to know each person as we'd discuss the details of the medical protocol, their testing results, and the roadblocks they experienced. I came to observe that the measurements and tests I was doing greatly influenced the client's emotions and motivation, and we would end up talking more about their issues with food and the discontent they had with their body than with the actual protocol.

The hardest part of the protocol, despite the potential physical benefits, was getting people to follow it. As much as I approached the hCG protocol as a hormonal therapy for the body, the people doing it were highly emotional about it, *as if it was more about proving their worth than it was about improving their health.* Most people were doing it as a way to fix their poor self-esteem, which made them emotional about the physical results. I observed that the intentions of the client and the way they viewed the process changed his or her response to both the limitations of the protocol as well as the physical results. Because I believed the client's motivation to follow the protocol was imperative to getting accurate results, as well as a truthful understanding of the potential physical benefits, my interest shifted from *the physiology of the process to the emotional aspects that made it difficult for people to follow the protocol. I observed that when people were emotional about the weight loss, they struggled:*

- To discern physical hunger and satiation, making the protocol very difficult for them to follow.

- With obsessive monitoring of their size and weight. How

they reacted to the change directly impacted their willingness to follow the protocol.

- With emotional desires to eat. They'd reason and rationalize not adhering to the protocol despite not being hungry and risking the potential physical benefits the protocol
could provide.

- To accept the natural results of the protocol, despite significant physical improvements.

- With fear about weight gain and reintroducing food once
the protocol was over, making them increasingly obsessed
with their weight and food.

- With increased emotional eating and binge eating the
more they feared food after the protocol was over.

I found that my past experience with an eating disorder and my miraculous
recovery kept coming up as I'd recognize how they were feeling and how
that impacted their relationship with food. It was as if I was witnessing my
past thoughts, impulses, and behavior in some variation in every person I
observed. As I met with each person and his or her issues would arise, I'd
attempt to give them insight based on the recollection of my own recovery,
and it would help.

This was very difficult because I'd put my disorder and recovery on a shelf—
and to help others I had to bring it all back up to the forefront of my mind.
These were things I hadn't thought about in over a decade. To me, it was a
past life that didn't need to be processed, rethought, or discussed. I was free,
and had no reason to rehash my previous disorder and recovery. However,
the more I interacted with patients through the medical protocol, the more
my previous suffering and recovery came up.

Because I could relate, I could help verbalize much of what they were experiencing, whereas by themselves they didn't have words to describe or explain it.

Weight-Loss Apocalypse and YouTube Sessions

As I met with more and more people, I found that the issues they struggled with became more and more predictable. As well, some common roadblocks and questions consistently came up. To answer these questions and to show how I coached people through roadblocks, I started a YouTube channel. Through videos, I shared with followers the process I describe in *Weight-Loss Apocalypse, Books 1 and 2.* I posted full sessions showing me talking with clients as I prepared them for the hCG protocol, as well as follow-up sessions discussing roadblocks and emotional issues with food and their body.

My experience with an eating disorder came up consistently as I tried to help explain what I was observing in these clients. Over the course of a couple of years, people from all over the globe found my YouTube channel and started reaching out for my help. Gradually, as the clients struggled with more intense issues, the content of my posted sessions shifted away from the hCG protocol to being focused on emotional eating, body image, the diet industry, and eating disorders.

Today I've helped hundreds of people from all over the world who have suffered with issues from across the spectrum of eating disorders.

As more and more people diagnosed with eating disorders reached out to me to talk, the more I've been challenged to understand my own recovery.

I've had to revisit my past trauma, past depression, and the darkness of the eating disorder I was trapped by in order to be able to help others express and describe what they are experiencing. I've also had to recall my own recovery, and to find words to explain and give context to what I experienced. It has taken me years working with hundreds of people, as well as countless hours studying, to have a bigger grasp on the issue that goes beyond my own personal experience, and even today, I struggle to communicate it properly. In 2019, I published my full story in *My Weight-Loss Apocalypse: Rebirth from the Ashes of Eating Disorder Hell.* My story is available to purchase from my website at: https://WeightLossApocalypse.com

You will find throughout the *Thin-Supremacy* series of books that I reference my experience with an eating disorder, as well as my recovery. It is very difficult to explain what it feels like, and the way a person thinks when they have an eating disorder, unless you have fully recovered. This is why I consistently describe my experience and use myself as an example. It can help the reader find a sense of understanding, get relief and be able to relate.

My hope when I published *My Weight-Loss Apocalypse* was to describe my story and to give people context for where my awareness of eating disorders come from. *Again, I am not a licensed therapist, nor am I formally trained in psychology in any way.* Outside of a dietetics course specific to eating disorders I took one semester in college, my knowledge about the subject comes from personal experience, research, lots of reading, and from the ob servations I've made talking to people who've sought out my feedback.

My goal in writing the *Thin-Supremacy* series of books is to give those that connect with the content of my YouTube sessions more important information that might make sense of the work I'm doing. *If you are suffering from an eating disorder, but don't connect to the content I present, it probably isn't appropriate for your condition.* You should seek out help that is appropriate, and that offers you relief. Don't give up! There is sense in why you're suffering; you just need to find the reasons and seek out answers for what needs to change in order to bring you peace.

For those that connect, all I can give is insight. I don't have exact instructions. What I present here are my thoughts and what I've studied about the subject. These are my subjective observations, and if they help, great!

My hope is that eating disorders are looked at from a new angle, not as a disorder, but as a syndrome. My intent is to openly discuss the issues from a broader perspective, and to give insight to people that might help, in some way, to relieve their suffering. I don't promise recovery, but rather to open your mind and give you hope. Permanent recovery is possible. You might need to look at things differently, and that's what I hope to do: *to give you a different perspective.*

The Goals of the *Thin Supremacy* Book Series

This entire series of books was originally written as one book. As I realized it was too large and covered too wide a range of complex information for one book, I decided to split the information into four parts. I published each section as its own book, in order of the first *(Thin Supremacy)*, second *(Diet Supremacy)*, and third book *(Body Supremacy)*. These three books I call the *Thin Supremacy* series. The last section of the original book is the final book—Surrendering Your Survival. I see this book as the central cornerstone to the entire series—it provides the most important instructions toward recovery. The *Thin Supremacy* series is support for *Surrendering Your Survival*, and vice versa. They all work better together than they do separate.

A simple way to understand how these books work together is that the three *Thin Supremacy* series books were written as a way to observe eating disorders from an evolutionary psychological perspective, and to try to find sense in why people's relationship with their body and food can get so disordered. These books have more academic and intellectual content about eating disorders that is meant to be studied by people who are suffering, *and also by professionals who help people dealing with these issues.* However, intellect about the problem doesn't necessarily provide what's needed when it comes to letting your eating disorder go in order to get on the path toward recovery. *Surrendering Your Survival* is about letting go and getting on that path.

Surrendering Your Survival: A Conscious Path to Eating Disorder Recovery provides directions toward escaping the torments of eating disorder hell. In this book I speak from my own understanding of the torment and suffering of an eating disorder, and from my own experience escaping and recovery from it. I wrote *Surrendering Your Survival* to speak heart to heart with those who are inside the dark cage of their eating disorder. I articulate the survival terror experienced by those who are a prisoner to their disordered behaviors, and provide clarity about what it will take in order to willfully choose to surrender the safety that those behaviors supply. When reading this book, it will feel as if I'm sitting with you in that darkness, with compassion for why you are in such a state of terror and anguish, showing and describing the path you'll need to take in order to escape.

Surrendering Your Survival describes what will need to be sacrificed, what has to be accepted, and the price that must be paid to take the path that leads to recovery. I give the reader a look into what recovery feels like, a method guided by the body to relearn a functional way to eat, and send a message of hope to those who are seeking freedom from an eating disorder.

Thin Supremacy: Body Image and Our Cultural Battle with Weight focuses and discusses the underlying psychological mechanisms and societal belief systems that encourages people to reinforce unrealistic body images. For people who internalize these images, they are more likely to experience feelings of shame when their body is different. This shame is a primary motivation for why people diet and why people eat emotionally. I believe emotional eating issues are just a symptom, projected out from mechanisms meant to protect life, coming from the desire to "fit in" and feel lovable through body image.

Diet Supremacy: The Toxic Bond Between Shame, Dieting, and Emotional Eating describes the survival mechanisms that are triggered as the struggle to accept body fat promotes an anxiety-ridden conflict between dieting—and the survival urges to gain access to food and to eat in self-defense. I believe the cognitive distortions about one's body and food, like dysmorphia, perfectionism, and all-or-nothing thinking, are from a clash between the psychological drive to belong, fit in, and be accepted—and the more vital, more important need to survive with food.

Body Supremacy: Exploring the Torment of Eating Disorders as a Syndrome goes deeper into the mind and darkness of eating disorders. This book discusses the possibility that eating disorders might be more of a syndrome, where compliance is a form of self-preservation necessary to survive in narcissistic cultures where codependency and trauma bonding might be more prevalent. I believe people who suffer with an eating disorder hold themselves to abusive and inhumane controls—like someone with Stockholm Syndrome—because they believe that's what's required in order to earn safety, acceptance, and love from the narcissistic supremacy (their captor) that has power and control over their survival needs.

These books are not "light reading." The content and information presented is meant to help the reader to see things from a different point of view. For this to happen, you might need to read, study, cross reference, and reread different chapters from each book in the series. From a change in perspective, the goal is to see from a larger vantage point, to think differently, and to ask questions that might have uncomfortable answers.

If you are looking for light and easy reading, these books are not for you. If you are seeking answers, explanations and heart-felt care and concern, these books ARE for you.

SECTION 1

Survival Mode and the Threat of Danger

"How can a single human cell measuring 1/1000 of an inch across contain instructions within its DNA that would fill 1000 books with 600 pages each? The more we learn about the workings of the body, the more we realize just how vast is the intelligence at work within it, and how little we know. When the mind reconnects with that, it becomes a most wonderful tool. It then serves something greater than itself."

– Eckhart Tolle, *The Power of Now*

Primitive survival mechanisms that are geared to distort the way we think should be the center of any discussion when observing body image and thin(ner) supremacy—chiefly how these concepts distort the way people relate to their body and to food, further triggering primitive survival mechanism specific to feeding behavior.

Because these subjects are imperative when you look at eating disorders as a syndrome, I've copied and condensed parts of what's written in *Diet Supremacy,* and combined them to form the first and second chapters of this book. This content is a reminder of what survival mode is, psychologically how humans have evolved to prioritize survival needs, and how insecurity with those needs impacts the way we think.

It is my intent to present this extremely complex topic of survival in a way that helps you grasp how it relates dieting, emotional eating, disordered eating, and eating disorders. My hope is that you can see the forest for the trees and have more compassion for your own humanness, as well as the suffering of others struggling to survive.

To the Reader: Before You Start…

To start, the content of this book is meant for readers who want to get a deeper look into eating disorders—and from a different perspective. The way I look at eating disorders isn't as an "expert." I do not have the education and appropriate study to claim such a title. With that said, the way I look at eating disorders is from the perspective of a person who has suffered directly *while being inside the insanity of one,* but also from the vantage point of someone who's experienced complete and instantaneous relief with a full and total recovery.

> **I am not an eating disorder expert, but I am a direct witness of what it feels like, how the mind works in it, and what it took to escape.**

In this book, I will not be presenting the specific details of what defines an eating disorder. This information can be found in other books, online, and with psychiatric professionals that more fully grasp the specific symptoms that differentiate one disorder from another. I will be discussing the aspects of eating disorders that, *from my perspective,* not only brought on the greatest severity of suffering, but were also the most important when it came to my recovery.

I will be presenting an idea that looks at eating disorders—viewing them as a syndrome—and in doing so will be examining information that might not be of interest to these people: 1) those who don't suffer from these horrible limitations, 2) who don't know someone suffering with these issues, or 3) who don't help others who are in agony trying to recover.

This book would be of interest to a reader who wants to study and understand the twisted mindset of people holding themselves hostage inside the darkness of an eating disorder. You'll learn what keeps them delusional about what defines safety and danger. This is for readers who want to understand why people would clutch onto something that is killing them—and do so with their entire identity and purpose in life.

If you as the reader are looking for something more lighthearted to read, this book and the entire *Thin-Supremacy* series is not for you. If you're looking to study and better understand the complex issues that underly body image, emotional eating, obsessive dieting, disordered eating, and eating disorders—*this series of books might be what you're looking for.*

Chapter 1

The Terror Inside an Eating Disorder

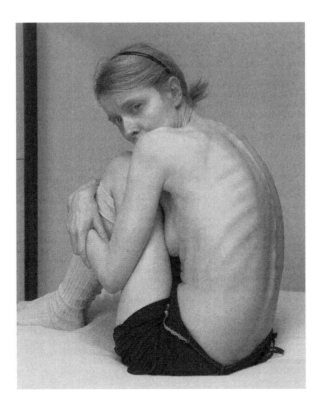

"Fear doesn't exist anywhere except in the mind."

– Dale Carnegie, author

Request for my help from an 18-year-old woman:
Hello Robin, I am a recent high school graduate who is enrolled in college in the fall. I have been watching your videos on YouTube for about a year now, and it has really helped me in understanding the nature of my disorder.

I have been bulimic for about four years now (writing that just now really shocked me), but I believe my eating disorder began in sixth grade when I started dieting (starving) myself and the goal of losing weight took hold of my life.

I have been in therapy before, but I felt that none of the therapists truly understood the issue, at least with the clarity you had. The therapist I've been going to had her recovery plan based on a food-centered model, so the focus was on forced feeding and making sure I ate enough food every day. But after listening to you and experiencing the freedom of not caring for a moment, I loathed going back to the idea of planning or even thinking about what I had to eat again. Besides, this was the issue I wanted to get rid of in the first place!

It's been about 3 months since I last saw this therapist and I thought I could do this on my own, yet I'm in the same place and still struggling. I feel as if I'm on the brink of permanently detaching myself from these beliefs on thinness. I am allowing myself intervals of freedom with food; however, I am still struggling to completely abandon my desire to be thinner. I do not want to continue this, and I just wish to speak to someone who can understand the issue I have with thinness.

When "Feeling Fat" Feels Like Terror

For me, gaining fat felt like getting murdered. I experienced an extreme terror, which is why I went to such drastic and abusive measures to defend myself by doing whatever necessary to maintain my leanness. Any other person with the same level of impending fear of being murdered attached to weight gain would do the same thing. I never would have thought my desire to be thinner was the problem.

When I talk with other people who have disordered eating, or eating disorders, they too have similar fear and with similar terror-like intensity. It doesn't start that way, which is why it's hard to identify.

> **You wouldn't suspect something as innocent as wanting to be thinner as being dangerous.** *But when that desire is backed by primitive survival needs that make your body and food the enemy, it's not safe or innocent at all.*

Insecure survival needs distort and magnify anything it latches onto, making seemingly simple and ordinary ideas into radicalized notions. And as those notions become less and less flexible and more and more rigid, survival mechanisms gradually distort notions into zealotry and dogma.

In terms of thin(ner) supremacy, fatter conditions of the body become a predatory threat to life, and the mind then responds accordingly. When you "feel" fat you are actually feeling threat, as if you are easy prey to a predator.

I recall this is what feeling "fat" felt like:

- It started with a dark, impending doom, and my body would involuntarily respond.

- I'd feel a flash of heat, my breathing felt compressed, and I'd start to sweat.

- My heart would beat so fast and hard it felt like it was going to come out of my chest.

- My hair would stand up on end.

- My stomach would hurt, and I'd feel nauseous, and it felt as if I was going to explode if something wasn't done immediately.

- My thoughts became erratic, like being short-circuited, and I couldn't think straight.

- It felt as if I was seeing through tunnel vision.

- My entire mind and body had an intense urgency to do something *now*.

- A horrible threat was there, and I needed to escape *right now*—as if there was extreme danger or emergency.

Each and every person I've worked with has described similar sensations. For some people, the feelings of impending doom or peril come when she feels deprived of food, and the only way to get rid of that horrible feeling is to eat. For others, threat is attached to gaining weight, which is why she micro-manages food and exercises obsessively. Like me, some people experience this impending doom with both food restriction and gaining weight, which is why they obsessively diet, and compulsively binge and then purge.

This has brought me to ponder the influence that both the fight-or-flight response and the controlling nature of sus-

tained survival mode have on body image, disordered eating, and eating disorders.

Survival Mode

Survival mode is hard-wired physiological, psychological, and behavioral mechanisms triggered by apparent insecurity to handle perceived, or actual dangerous threats. In terms of how survival mode functions psychologically, it directs your thoughts and focus inward, toward self-preservation.

- This mode of existence is emotionally and physically geared toward securing safety, removing risk, and responding to threat with forceful life-preserving and death-avoiding behavior.

- These involuntary mechanisms have evolved over tens of thousands of years—of running or hiding from predators, surviving and preparing for famine, and fighting threats to keep ourselves and our loved ones safe from harm or death.

- The sensitive response to apparent dangers, and preventative forecast of threat, has become so important to the survival of our species that this mode is activated even if the threat is simply suspected or perceived.

- Survival mode can be triggered even if you experience something as simple as the stress felt when facing a situation in life you feel challenged to handle.

- Danger doesn't have to actually exist.

Apparent danger initiates the sympathetic nervous system, which is part of the brain, spinal cord, and nerves that regulate unconscious or automatic functions like heartbeat, temperature, digestions, etc.

When the nervous system is stimulated by perceived threat:

- It turns on or encourages organs that are necessary to promote optimal physical exertion.

- The pupils in your eyes dilate.

- The adrenals release the hormones *cortisol and adrenalin,* both involved in energizing the body with increased heart rate and respiration. This also raises the hair on the body.

- It also breaks down energy stored in the liver to release sugar into the blood stream as immediate fuel for the muscles.

- Blood vessels constrict, altering the distribution of blood away from the abdomen toward the heart, lungs, central nervous system, and the limbs.

At the same time there is resistance, reduced stimulus, or depression of non-important functions during threat. The mouth dries, the gut and intestines immediately stop producing digestive enzymes, peristalsis or contractions of the digestive systems halts, and hunger goes away. Some people experience nausea, or a burning sensation in the stomach. The more intense the perceived danger, the more intense the physiological response and the longer the body stays this way.[1] This means that the more fear you experience, the more and the longer the body responds.

For survival mechanisms to be initiated, the threat of danger must be intuited, meaning it is perceived and understood. Then the body responds accordingly. Think of a time you've watched a scary movie and it left you too scared to fall asleep at night. Your body responds to perceived danger exactly the same as it would in true danger. Contraction of your blood vessels result in "a cold sweat," the mouth dries, hair raises, the heart beats rapidly, breathing increases, muscles tremble and twitch, the pupils of the eyes dilate, and the sense to do something immediately magnifies.[1]

Much of the science studying the physical and psychological reactions to potential threat was done in the late 1800s and early 1900s by scientists, such as the physiologist, Dr. Ivan Pavlov (1849–1936). Most people recognize him from his studies regarding conditioning, and how the dog's mouth watered when Pavlov rang a bell. But Pavlov also studied how the dog's digestion and salivation completely stopped when there was stress or agitation. Another renowned scientist from Harvard, Dr. Walter B. Cannon (1871–1945), studied the physiological response to perceived threat, fear, and anger. His work was foundational to the understanding of how we physically respond to perceived threats against our survival through what he describes as "fight or flight."

These fundamentals of survival-mode physiology were discussed and published in 1927 by Dr. Walter B. Cannon in his book, *Bodily Changes in Pain, Hunger, and Rage.* He found that when presented with a perceived or actual threat, our body goes through a series of physiological changes that prepare our body to either have the strength and endurance to fight for our lives— or to freeze or run and flee in order to hide, shrink, or attempt to disappear from threat.[1]

> **MY EXPERIENCE:** *Much of what Dr. Cannon describes in his book is exactly what I experienced when I suffered with an eating disorder. The fear response experienced when I believed I was gaining weight, and when I ate "bad" food, was as he described: tunnel*

vision (dilated pupils), rapid heart rate, cold sweats, hair standing up, dry mouth, and the urge to immediately do something physical.

When I was around food, especially "bad" food or food I felt deprived of, the fear that I couldn't control or handle my urges to eat, immediately triggered this fight-or-flight response, as if I was in a room with a dangerous enemy. At the same time, I'd have an intense desire to taste the food, eat it, and allow myself some grace to enjoy it. It was at this point that I'd either micro-manage every detail of the food in order to stay safe, or I'd negotiate with my fear to eat in a way that didn't seem as dangerous. "If I have only two bites, then I'm still safe." Or "If I puke, or exercise, then there's no danger." In a way, these negotiations reduced the perception of threat, which temporarily felt good or safe. But once I took a bite, things changed rapidly, and I'd lose my grip on safety. It was like thinking I'm going to take a couple of drinks from a fresh spring to quench a dehydrated craving for water, but finding that I'm teetering on the edge of a raging river, and have fallen in and was being pulled down a horrendous current I couldn't escape.

Food simultaneously became both life-saving and life-threatening.

Like anybody else, I did what I had to in order to hide or to suppress that feeling. Dieting prevented it, eating off plan promoted it, bingeing relieved it, feeling I was gaining weight promoted it, and purging or exercise relieved it. The cycle of dieting, eating, bingeing, purging, and dieting again ran through my mind over and over again.

This is exactly what I experienced, sometimes over ten times a day, which is why with an eating disorder my entire day was hijacked by whatever it took to feel safe and protected. Keep in mind that the amount of exhaustive work of micromanaging food, bingeing and purging, as well as the intense exercise regimens, didn't give me a sense of accomplishment. It's what was required just to feel safe or "normal," and to feel removed from terror. The eating disorder was both my fight and flight, but also my dangerous threat.

As food restrictions became more and more rigid, the terror around food intensified. The more catastrophic eating off my plan became, the bigger the binges got. The worse the terror became, the more impulsive I needed to purge or exercise. Imagine having a feeling that you are about to get killed, and the only way to feel safe is to binge, not eat even though you are hungry, or to eat but puke up your food, while all the world around you is eating freely, safely, without torment, horror, or obsession.

That's what it feels like to have an eating disorder. You're stuck in terror and extreme survival mode against your body and food, as both are necessary to survive.

Once I realized these feelings came from survival mechanisms, it gave me relief to know I wasn't crazy, but rather doing exactly what anybody else would do under the circumstance. Because food threatened my body image, and my body image threatened access to food, my mind lived in a constant state of fear, anxiety, with the need for controlling behaviors that stemmed from mechanisms derived from survival mode. I was in a constant state of fight and flight. Fighting for food, hiding from weight gain. Fighting weight gain, hiding from food. It was a vicious cycle between two separate survival needs competing with each other.

You and Your "Danger Probe"

In order for survival mode to be triggered, there first must be a signal that there's a dangerous threat. According to *Oxford Living Dictionary*, a "threat" is a person or thing *likely* to cause damage or danger, or the *possibility* of trouble, danger, or ruin. The keywords here are "likely" and "possibility." Threat doesn't have to be guaranteed to create a biological response in the body. It only has to be a *perceived possibility,* which means any threat you think could happen can alert the brain and nervous system, and trigger a degree of survival mode.

It's as if the brain has a "danger probe" attached to it, like an invisible antenna that is geared like a telescope to seek and detect vulnerability or potential danger.

This probe magnifies and surveys the environment, people, their body language, and any situation, animal, or bug that memory has recorded "as dangerous." Perceptions of threat initiate the physical mechanisms necessary to react in stress, whether it's to freeze in panic, hide in insecurity, run away (flight), or fight in self-defense. *The belief that you're too weak to handle threat, even if there is no actual present danger, alerts the mind to be on guard and to find any possible risk.*

- The sensitive response to apparent dangers has become so important to the survival of our species that our "danger probe" specifically seeks weakness and vulnerabilities and "looks out" for risk.

- Survival mode can be triggered even if you experience something as simple as the stress felt when facing a situation in life you feel challenged to handle. Physical danger doesn't have to actually exist.

- Even if you're strong enough to handle a threat, but you don't think you are, the belief that you're not capable is more powerful. The mind interprets assumption of weakness and inadequacy as real and true.

A person's "danger probe" must first know what defines danger in order to detect and seek it out. This involves a two-part comparison of 1) oneself in relation to 2) one's environment. These perceptions merge in the mind to assess "threat." [1, 2]

As described by Dr. Joseph E LeDoux, a renowned scientist and author who studies the brain and the fear response:

> *"The meaning of the environmental stimuli present is added by the retrieval of memories. If the stimuli are known sources of danger, 'fear' schema are retrieved from memory. My hypothesis, then, is that the feeling of 'fear' results when the outcome of these various processes (attention, perception, memory, arousal) coalesce in consciousness and compel one to feel 'fear.' This can only happen in a brain that has the cognitive wherewithal to have the concept of 'me,' or what Endel Tulving has called 'autonoetic consciousness.'"* [2]

A complex web of beliefs and memory about your capacity combine together to then be evaluated against your environment, circumstance, or situation, resulting in a stress signal that defines the level of threat or danger you're facing. Because of the variability in both self-evaluation as well as situational and environmental circumstance, fear isn't an all-or-nothing response. It works more like vol-

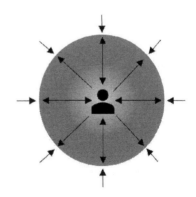

PERCEIVED THREAT

Results from a comparison of oneself in relation to apparent danger.

ume control, and can go up and down based on the perception of one's vulnerability.

The more dangerous the threat, combined with more insecurity within yourself, the higher grade of danger will be alarmed, resulting in higher intensity of survival mechanisms being triggered.

I assume that for most people, these are not conscious decisions. In the case of my eating disorder, my fear of fat gain was extreme—for reasons I didn't question or understand.

MY EXPERIENCE: *This level of fear would be considered radical, like a phobia. A phobia is a state of extreme fear typified by absolute avoidance of the feared object or event. I clearly didn't have a sense of being able to survive it, as gaining body fat represented certain death. It's as if my danger probe's power and volume was turned way up, magnifying its detecting and seeking sensitivity, making small things seem big in order to find any danger that posed the threat of fat gain.*

I was hypervigilant at exploring my body, and signally any sign of fat gain. I would grab my stomach, look in the mirror, weigh myself, and measure my waist with a measuring tape multiple times a day. The same occurred with my need to evaluate food and micromanage the content and calories of what I ate, as well as the calories I burned with exercise. These measures would make sense if there was in fact a threat of immediate death with each additional pound of body fat. However, what was driving the obsessive surveying of my body was the radical fear that my life was in grave danger because I couldn't handle what weight gain would do to my life.

Modes of Survival

Fight, flight, and freeze mechanisms involving the brain and nervous system respond to initial perceptions of the environment in response to memory from past experience, and self-awareness of one's capability. I imagine each survival-mode mechanism has a different perceptual trigger based on a person's sense of intrinsic competence and capacity to handle any given situation. For example:

- **Freeze:** When in a state of fear, shock and surprise, where there isn't a definitive understanding one way or the other of one's capacity, there might be a freeze response. This reaction would take mechanisms that are focused on being still, quiet, and shrinking one's self, to disappear into background. I assume that without action, this would be experienced as anxiety.

- **Strength to Fight:** When there is a sense of competence to change a threat, the urge would be to fight. Fighting would entail a degree of anger or a way to inflate oneself to seem bigger and better than he or she naturally is. This takes a degree of pride, work, and physical energy to exert force. The end goal is being better, stronger, and superior to any threat.

- **Stamina to Run Away:** When there's some confidence but less energy, a more passive way to fight would be to run away or flee the scene. The stamina of mechanisms geared to deny, avoid, repress, procrastinate, place blame, or distract from vulnerable situations would be needed to separate oneself from threat. Over time this would be fatiguing and depressing.

- **Adaption to Hide:** When there's lack of confidence in oneself, but stronger confidence in one's surrounding or systems, he or she might be inclined to hide or "blend in." Energy is directed toward taking in information about one's environment. An alternative mechanism would be to work hard ahead of time to prevent perceived threats.

The Need for a Shield, Weapon, and Armor

The ultimate goal of survival mechanisms is to stay alive. Therefore, if a person feels inadequate within themselves, they are more likely to seek out assistance or help elsewhere. It would make sense to protect yourself by obtaining a shield or weapon in order to handle danger that you feel inferior to handle. For example, imagine backpacking through the wilderness, knowing that you're easy prey to certain predatory animals. With a taser, knife, pepper spray, or a gun, the capacity to handle those dangers in the wilderness would increase, therefore decreasing your perceptions of threat and the fear response.

When protective armor, a weapon, shield, or tool is used to reduce the threat a danger poses, the relationship with that tool can seem like a life-or-death matter. The same risk of danger can be signaled if that survival need is vulnerable and could be taken away. For example, when it comes to survival requirements to stay alive, it would make sense that anything that threatens your ability to gain access to food and water would trigger danger.

For people suffering with an eating disorder, both bingeing and excessive food consumption can be used as a shield from vulnerability in life, more so when food restrictions are what triggers the feeling of danger. For people who use lean, fit, and "healthy" body images like armor and use exercise and dieting as a shield, it would feel dangerous to let those things go. When I suffered with an eating disorder, my anxiety went up when I didn't exercise. Without controlling my food, anxiety felt like terror. Without the ideal body image, it felt like my life wouldn't exist.

Message from a YouTube follower:
I'm in my 20's and I was molested by my step-father from the age
of 6 to 13. I know it's not my fault, but I've always felt that some-
thing about me has attracted these problems. I need to address this.
I binge eat every meal and I hate my body. I want out, but I don't
know how to stop doing something that keeps me safe from life.

For someone suffering on the anorexic end of the eating disorder spectrum it might feel like this:

Fear of Not Dieting or Exercising = Fear of Body Fat = Fear of being exposed as inadequate = Fear of embarrassment = Fear of being criticized and being deemed worthless = Fear of being rejected and abandoned = Fear of living life alone = Fear you can't handle it = Fear of death.

For someone suffering on the binge-eating side of the eating disorder spectrum, it might feel like this:

Fear of having too much body fat = Fear of food = Fear of being exposed as too inadequate to handle life stress = Fear of not having enough food = Fear of having too much body fat = Fear of being exposed as worthless = Fear of being criticized and shamed = Fear of being rejected and abandoned = Fear of living life alone = Fear you can't handle it = Fear of death.

The fear of body fat most likely stems from fear of judgment that then triggers warnings of abandonment, which stems from fear of being alone—

and being alone would be a problem only if you didn't think you could provide essential life needs, such as food, water, and shelter for yourself…or if you didn't feel capable of creating your own joy in life.

> **Ultimately, all of these fears stem from evolutionary wiring that presumes *you will die* without having what you've attached your security to.**

> **IMPORTANT:** Although the evaluation of one's capacity in relation to a potential danger, to some degree, makes the triggers of danger a personal experience, as human beings we have evolved to be predictable in what we evaluate ourselves by.

> **Through tens of thousands of years, we've evolved to be "pre-wired" to feel increasingly insecure with more vital needs to survive. When you're vulnerable, these needs determine the priority of our psychological motivations.**

Evolutionary psychology suggests, as humans have evolved physically to survive the environment, we've also evolved psychologically with *the drive and desire to get what we need to stay alive and to avoid death.* It would make sense that our minds are pre-wired with "genetic memory" then, to be attracted to and defensive of necessary life requirements that would improve our capacity to survive.

It's predictable that humans have some degree of insecurity when seen as inadequate or worthy of exclusion—but based on findings, we have higher degrees of insecurity when it comes to losing shelter and environmental safety, and we are the most insecure to handle threats to food, water, shelter and other physiological necessities for life.

The innate drive and motivation of human behavior—looked at from the angle of evolutionary psychology—is largely based on the work of world-renowned scientist, Dr. Abraham Maslow (1908–1970). According to his research studying human motivation and behavior, our foremost psychological priority is to secure the most important things needed to stay alive. In terms of our innate "danger probe," he believed our probe was prewired to seek danger and threat to the most vital physiological needs for life, like food, more so than other needs.

As it relates to eating disorders, it would be predictable that a person who perpetually diets or believes food is going away would suffer from chronic survival mechanisms and cognitive distortions geared to focus on food.

Maslow's observations went beyond being hunted by a tiger and chased by a bear. He observed that the loss of what's needed to survive is equally as threatening, and he eventually created a hierarchy of survival needs.

Request for my help from a woman in her late 20's:
I'm 27 years old and am currently battling Binge Eating Disorder. I have been struggling with body image and various eating disorders for about eight years. Right now, I am at the most hopeless and desperate place I've ever been in my life. Watching your videos has been a tremendous help, but I think I would really benefit from your help to make that final transition and move forward from this addiction.

"In obedience there is always fear, and fear darkens the mind."

– Jiddu Krishnamurti, Philosopher

Chapter 2

Evolutionary Psychology and Maslow's Lower Hierarchy of Survival Needs

MASLOW'S HIERARCHY OF NEEDS

"Fear, rage, and pain, and the pangs of hunger are all primitive experiences which human beings share with the lower animals. These experiences are properly classed as among the most powerful that determine the action of men and beasts. A knowledge of the conditions which attend these experiences, therefore is of general and fundamental importance in the interpretation of behavior."

– Dr. Walter B. Cannon, *Bodily Changes in Pain, Hunger, Fear, and Rage*

Evolutionary Psychology, Survival Mode, and Maslow's Hierarchy of Survival Needs

Dr. Abraham Maslow's pivotal work described our fundamental psychological drives being based on securing the most important life-and-death needs. Dr. Maslow is best known for what is called the "hierarchy of needs." He maintained that before anything else, our mind and psychological drive is motivated to first secure and to make safe the most important fundamental needs that keep us alive. Without these things, the probability of death goes up. Not because you're being attacked, but because having less control over those requirements leaves us powerless to stay alive.

Anything that gets in the way of our personal ability to obtain vital needs on a daily basis, alerts and activates our "danger probe," triggers the vulnerability of death, and initiates a sense of potential threat. Necessities that are less important get pushed out of focus as the mind closes to harness all attention and energy to point in a singular direction toward seeing only those critical needs.

What's experienced is agitation and badness that motivates, through tunnel vision, all focus and thoughts toward doing whatever is necessary to get relief by obtaining and securing the pleasure and gratification of those critical life needs.

Once those needs are secure, then our mind can open and be relieved from the self-centered focus and nature of "survival mode" to prioritize additional, but less-important survival needs.

Based on Maslow's Hierarchy of Needs, you could say our psychological "danger probe" is more sensitive to the most critical survival needs and not as much to the less-important survival needs. Maslow's pyramid gives a visual representation of what he theorized was the largest triggers to survival mode at the bottom (food, water, shelter, belonging) and freedom from survival mode as you move toward the top (exploration, spiritual endeavor, enlightenment, etc.).

The end goal would be to secure these most important survival needs so that our "danger probe" can be turned way down, in order to relax our mind and widen our perspective. This opening of the mind liberates the energy of our existence to explore and experience the freedom needed to be curious and create what we want with our lives.

> **NOTE:** In this book, I will be describing the lower, more-controlling hierarchy of needs. The upper, more-liberated hierarchies will be addressed when I discuss recovery in *Surrendering Your Survival.*

Maslow's First Hierarchy of Needs: Physiological Requirements

The fundamental and most sensitive needs of survival are the most important conditions necessary physiologically in order to support the life of the body: food, water, clean air, sleep, etc. If these needs are threatened, insecure, or are not met, not only will you show signs of psychological stress, but the physical stress eventually ends in death. What Maslow found is that our mind involuntarily prioritizes focus, and magnifies the desire for these requirements if they are perceived as threatened, *more than any other need.*

> **The mind pushes less-important needs into the background, and brings forward all attention, motivation, and harnessed energy towards adequately securing these most important physical needs—to *above all else,* stay alive.**

For example, if your food supply quantity is perceived as not adequate to eat today, cannot be replenished, or if it is not safe to eat, the mind will devote all attention to and emphasize what needs to be done to secure it. It will magnify attention on what tools are necessary to find food for immediate and later needs, places to forage and hunt, and how to stockpile enough food so the mind can be released to prioritize other less-important needs.

> **EXAMPLE:** The clients I've talked with who describe the urges to binge, commonly explain the impulse as being overwhelming and that it takes over their mind and all of their thoughts. Only after they give in to the urge, and allow themselves to eat without restraint, does the incessant pressure and focus on eating go away.

It is obvious to me that people who suffer from the entire spectrum of eating disorders might be experiencing symptoms of this hierarchy of need—not feeling secure or in their control. If food supply is being threatened, the mind will obsess to some degree on what it takes to secure food to make it:

- Available now,
- Adequate in quantity to support immediate needs,
- Safe to eat,
- Replenishable and stockpiled, and
- Good to taste.

This is described in more detail in *Hierarchy of Food Needs,* by Registered Dietician, Elly Satter, MS, RD, LCSW, BCD. Satter detailed what needs must be met in order to secure this hierarchy of need. Until food is fully and completely secure, the mind will need to keep thoughts of food and eating at the front of the mind *at all times.* It's as if your food is being threatened, and the mind's eye must keep constant watch over it.[3] This is experienced through urges, thoughts, cravings, hunger pains, and fantasies about food.

Because of the vital requirement for our physiological needs, particularly food, our psychological mind is highly sensitive

to perceptions that food might be dangerous to eat, or access to it might be threatened, like in the case of famine or a food shortage.

Of course, feasting, stocking, and preserving food would be vital when preparing for famine. Even if the famine is artificial, meaning it is contrived as food is in fact abundant and accessible, these primitive impulses to feast still get triggered.

What is consciously experienced is:

- Incessant thoughts of food.

- Fantasies about the taste of forbidden food.

- A magnified awareness and thoughts of the "bad" food you're not supposed to eat.

- Increased sensitivity to the way food smells, and how food tastes.

- Mental fixation on when, what, and how much you've eaten and how much you'll get to eat later.

- Shame for being too weak to obey the authority that's been given to the diet.

Think of dieting as a superficially imposed artificial "famine." In essence, when a person restricts food, she is willfully attempting to create an equation that translates to food shortage, all while she has immediate access to overflowing abundance of food surrounding her. This is largely problematic because feeling we are deprived or withheld from food, and not having control over our access to food triggers hardwired psychologically survival impulses to eat in order to protect ourselves from of the threat of starvation.

It's as if your survival mind won't let you focus on any other things, except food. It's like a bear preparing for hibernation—until you surrender to those urges and feed the primal animal motivations to eat, you live in the tension between the intensifying agitation and angst restricting food and an increasing appetite for forbidden food. Until you believe eating is safe and secure from every angle, your mind will be devoted to it until it is. And when that happens, according to Maslow's theory, our mind and motivation can be released to think about other less-important needs, like the ability to protect ourselves from outside elements and potential predators.

Maslow's Second Hierarchy of Need: *Environmental Safety*

This need is geared to seek safety from the perceived threat to one's body, home, health, and ability to protect her space. It encompasses our territorial nature, and having a space we can call our own.

- Do you have a safe place to sleep?
- Do you have appropriate attire to keep you safe from environmental risks like weather, bugs, and disease?
- Do you have medicine or health care in case you or a loved one gets injured?
- Are you sheltered and protected from dangerous animals?
- Is your home safe, secure, and comfortable?

I recall after experiencing sexual assault while in college, I had this strong urge to clean, organize, and control my environment. It felt as if having my space hygienic and orderly would bring me a sense of peace, calm, and safety within myself. I assume this response was directly related to my desire to remove vulnerability from my life, and to feel safe in my own environment.

Similarly, I've had clients who were also obsessive about cleanliness, and experienced anxiety and agitation when their home wasn't orderly. Many people have described how on and off again they fixate on their clothing, makeup, and hair. They spend significantly more time and effort organizing, cleaning, and sterilizing their home, their car, and their clothing when they feel optimistic and energized. But during times they feel down, or feel like a failure, they let it all go. Based on Maslow's theory, this directly stems from motivation to fulfill a different hierarchy of need. When a bigger, more significant need requires attention, less important needs go to the wayside.

A great example of this need is often displayed in how people lean politically, and why people are equally as defensive and strongly opinionated about affordable health care. Having these survival needs fulfilled might satisfy important aspects of what people perceive brings them environmental security and safety, and ultimately improved overall psychological well-being. The need to feel safe in one's own environment is why having a job and secure housing is also so important.

I've observed that when a person struggles with job loss, injury, or significant change in her home life like moving, that her energy and motivation to diet diminishes greatly. This is a time many people jump off the diet wagon, going from all to nothing. The unnecessary strain and energy needed to restrict food seems ridiculous when life presents real-life stress—especially when the stress is coming from a threat to your ability to financially support your family, like a loss in income or the loss of a job. For some reason, people don't see that when dieting they are under survival stress, but when it comes to a threat to their job, or home life, they are consciously aware they are experiencing survival stress, and will even admit they are in "survival mode."

According the Maslow, once you feel you have security, safety, and protection from both perceived as well as real life-threatening environmental challenges, then energy, motivation, and focus can move up the hierarchy to more complex, but less necessary needs in order to sustain life. This includes relationships with others, and the desire to feel lovable, accepted, and to belong securely with family, friends, and also feel safe in your community.

Maslow's Third Hierarchy of Need: *Love and Belonging*

Maslow's third hierarchy of need encompasses the innate survival motivation to feel worthy of love and to be seen as a valuable member of one's community—and to have something to give, something to share, and something to add to the society. It also encompasses our instincts to avoid, deny, hide from, and prevent criticism, ridicule, embarrassment, guilt, and shame.

Maslow's third hierarchy of need is very important because when working functionally with others as a team to survive, the primary, more-important hierarchies of need, are more likely to be fulfilled.

Evolutionary psychologists theorize that our inherent drive to belong in a group stems from tens of thousands of years with dramatic improvements to survivability and safety that occurred when people lived in small groups, helping and working together as a team. Eventually, this evolved into a survival need, to the point that our motivation to "fit in," feel valued, and feel safe with others feels like a life-or-death matter.

Our brains have been wired to release pleasurable signals of safety when we have a purpose in the group, are accepted, needed, and loved. Conversely, our brains are also wired to experience withdrawal and negative irritating fight-or-flight signals when we perceive there is potential threats tied to being demoted or rejected. Those signals are more intense:

1) the more inadequate a person feels within herself, and

2) the more she needs her group to survive.

According to evolutionary psychology, our inborn drive to avoid rejection evolved in times of disease and scarcity to prioritize survival of the group over the survival of the individual. If there was food shortage or famine, the group would prioritize rations of food for those that contributed and were perceived as beneficial to the group. The sick and needy were stigmatized, given less food, and in dire situations, were abandoned to fend for themselves in the wilderness, which meant certain death. *Rejection, when survival is dependent on inclusion in your tribe, equates to death.*

> **As an evolved threat to survival, the perception of abandonment, or being worthy of abandonment, still triggers fight-or-flight mechanisms today, as if we continue to live in the wilderness and will die alone if we don't secure relationships with others.**

If someone important to you is disappointed in you, you aren't going to die, but emotionally it can feel catastrophic. When there's apparent threat of disapproval, the brain has warning mechanisms that are like loud sirens, bright flashing lights, and magnified threat signals that get triggered when something dangerous seems to be happening. Immediately, involuntary self-preserving defense mechanisms get activated, which is similar to if you were encountering a dangerous predator. You feel the urge to fight, freeze in your tracks, or run away and hide.

In the case of social condemnation, your perceived mistakes and the group's disapproval are the predator. In effect, when a person is radically insecure within herself, the need to be secure with family, friends, or community can take over all other survival needs.

A person's perceptions of being important to a group increases confidence in his or her survivability—that there's security in advance of threat or danger. In addition, as roles and relationships in a group become more predictable and secure, the capacity to explore, mate, and to innovate expands.

These benefits can give the impression that the *third hierarchy of need—to be included and belong—*is more important than the first and second hierarchy of needs. Although, as working with others brings increased capacity to survive, it also brings competition, shared resources, relationship and communication problems, and the risk for being judged and rejected.

You could say this need and motivation to belong is based on the fact that humans are similar to other pack animals, like dogs, that thrive when working together to support life. But this comes with the downside of being territorial, competitive, and with pecking orders when resources are insecure or scarce.

Perceptions of not being valued by others can feel terrible. Underneath those feelings are evolved fears you're at higher risk for uncontrollable death.

No different from dogs that act out when neglected and abused, we too function and survive better when we feel secure, can give and receive love, and experience a sense of purpose. For this reason, a great deal of psychological wiring that drives motivation is geared to preserve and defend ourselves from judgment, rejection, and abandonment.

"Fitting In" and Body Image

One of our hardwired survival instincts that is directly related to Maslow's third hierarchy of need, is the drive to "fit in" to our community and with our family. Evolutionary wise, this includes looking the part and blending into your culture. Our mind's survival "danger probe" seeks any information in our environment that might indicate safety or danger. One of the signals our survival mechanisms are probing for is *repetition*. Whether it's repeated danger or repeated safety, our mind is seeking to learn from consistency in order to predict what we'll experience in any given environment. *Repetition equates to safety.*

Humans are dominantly visual beings, and the ability to not stick out as visually different is considered a vital safety mechanism, particularly in environments that feel vulnerable to danger. Imagine traveling to a foreign country where their common dress code is dramatically different than what you are wearing. It would be instinctive to feel the urge to purchase new clothing that would allow you to blend into their culture, so you don't stick out as an obvious outsider.

The survival illusion is that the more you see repeated images, especially consistent pictures associated with safety, the more likely you are to feel the urge and desire to adapt to that image.

When you consider how you feel about your physique, your conclusions are probably based on comparing your body to images repeated and seen in public, with your friends and family, and commonly on TV and social media.

This type of *social comparison* is how people come to understand if they "fit in."

> **NOTE:** In 1954, Leon Festinger, a social psychologist, proposed that when a person can't find a fair or objective understanding of how she "fits in," she often compares herself to others in order to fulfill the basic human drive for self-evaluation.[4]
>
> The more often people see repeated glamourized and promoted images of the body, the more likely they are to compare themselves to those images to assess their acceptability.[4]
>
> The goal is to not stand out as different, especially if different equates to being seen as bad or inferior. Not fitting in would feel as if you aren't worthy of inclusion, aren't welcome or trustworthy, and might end up being an outcast.

Our minds are wired to relax as we see repetition and consistency in how people look. Therefore, the more often you see images of the same type of body repeated over and over again, your mind unconsciously perceives the image as safe and "attractive." This is the premise of body image.

The traditional understanding of body image is that it is an internalized mental image of the body a person identifies by and wants, typically represented by what is perceived as safe or seen positively by others. *The idea is that a positively seen body reflects a positive inner-self.* It's as though the state of the body—its function, its looks, and other people's opinion about it—symbolizes safety from rejection and abandonment. Essentially, body image is an image of inclusion and an aspect of our third hierarchy of survival needs.

> **Ultimately, the image of the body that is repeated the most in a positive way represents acceptance, fitting in, and freedom from misery and death.**

Many people I work with describe feeling detached from their body, as if they can't inhabit it until it is "good enough." The goal they are chasing is to get their body to a predetermined state that they think when it's achieved, they will feel confident in their body, which will open up life to be lived in—safe from judgment, ridicule, and abandonment.

For a person to achieve that physical state, she must first internalize a concept of what determines right and correct in her mind, to which she agrees with and then compares her body to. That comparison dictates how she defines her relationship with her body in a positive or negative way, and then concludes if it's safe to be inhabited and accepted. It's a matter of conforming the body to a suitable image that "fits in" to the world she wants freedom to live in.

Today, the superior state of the body most people are pursuing is one that has minimal body fat. Over the past few generations, body-image standards of leanness have become so ingrained as being "unquestionable truth" that no one questions their validity. Worshipping and promoting the thinner ideal has become dogmatic.

The belief is that you should persist to be thinner than you naturally are, even if it isn't realistic for your body. No matter how much weight you've lost, you could still lose more. Even if it is only five more pounds—you aren't thin enough.

> **I call this dogma "thin supremacy," or "thinner supremacy," that is: no matter what, *you could always be thinner, and thinner is always better.***

The same concept of supremacy could apply to health, fitness, sexual attractiveness, or any other body image that is seen as ideal.

Message from 48-year-old professional woman and mother of two:
My culture is obsessed with physical appearance, and all my life and even as an adult I've heard, "Remember no one loves a fat girl but her mommy." Since I was a small child, I was told I was fat. Now when I look back at pictures of myself, I get so pissed off because I wasn't even a fat kid, I was normal. I went to private schools where most of the people where Caucasian. At that time, I thought I had to weigh 110 lbs. to fit in and be liked, like the skinny girls in my school.

Looking back, I realize to be that weight would have required I be emaciated. I always thought had so much weight to lose that it overwhelmed me. This is when I started emotional eating. In high school

I was a size 10–12. I thought I was so ugly all my life, despite strangers stopping me for no reason to tell me how beautiful I was. If a boy liked me, I thought there was something wrong with him, and I always was waiting for it to be a prank. It's been thirty years, and I'm still suffering. I need help.

The Mirage of Thin(ner) Supremacy

Based on Maslow's third hierarchy of need, it would be understandable why a person perceived as different, inferior, or "unsafe" would want to change the way she looks, and try to imitate others so that she doesn't stand out, seem threatening, or draw negative attention to herself. Mechanisms that direct energy and focus toward securing one's safety, get harnessed toward memorizing, learning, and consuming as much information as possible to become what is predictably valued in society.

The downside of this type of harnessed focus is that it ensures a person will know far more about cultural ideals than she does her innate and truthful human qualities.

Today—when there's more body acceptance and diversity shown than in the past—more often than not, images of idealized people portrayed in the media are air brushed and unnaturally distorted. For women, arms are thinned out. For men, arms are made more muscular. Necks and legs are extended, butts, boobs, and lips are magnified, waists are carved out to be thinner, and hair is made to look thicker, etc.

These repeated images are often paired with narcissistic symbolism, inferring they are the ultimate superior body types— and having that body type will make you appear superior, too.

The goal represented is to acquire a "positive body image." For this reason, the majority of people who repeatedly see *and imagine that these images are attainable* will assume their body, in comparison, is inadequate. Many "normal" or larger people feel a sense of danger about their size and weight, particularly women who compare themselves to consistent images in the media of people pictured who are considered 20 percent underweight.[5]

Without examining the body-image concept being sold, total power over whether a person can accept his or her body is given to businesses pushing ideas of health and inclusion that more often than not, are figments of the imagination. And I suspect these figments can be traced back to people who could arguably be analyzed as sociopaths or malignant narcissists who seek authoritarian control and power over others.

Unfortunately, followers naively trust these concepts as if it's their life purpose to achieve, and that the body shown to them is who they are. The body image becomes their identity, and how they understand their worth to society. For some people, instead of living their life open to learning, exploration, and creativity, they get trapped by their devotion to a body image, thinking someday it will be "good enough."

As someone accepts and internalizes the body-image concept of thin(ner) supremacy, it then becomes an unnoticeable personal belief. What is noticed, however, is that a person who is fatter isn't viewed with as much value as the thinner person who is automatically given a higher standing. You won't notice that the thinner ideal is 1) why you feel bad about your body, 2) why you think people who are thinner are more attractive and valuable, or 3) why you also yearn to be thinner.

**A person assumes excess weight is what she's battling, but
what she doesn't see is the desire for the internalized ideal she
judges her body by—*that is instigating this battle.***

People don't realize that many of these body-images being pushed as "positive" are based on unrealistic *delusions of grandeur*. Believers end up with a "negative body image," thinking their body must be made "positive" before they can accept the life that body provides them.

Like chasing a mirage, followers think that when they are thinner, they can relax and finally feel safe with, and accept their body. But for most people the ideal body image often demands insane forms of physical and psychological sacrifice that must be sustained in order for the goal to be maintained.

**The effort put into achieving these narcissistic body-image
standards are far beyond what any human should be expected
to do, just to feel safe and worthy of inclusion.**

When the vulnerability of life is accepted and survival mode put to rest, the way our mind works is to be less self-centered, biased, and self-promoting, and to be more open minded and exploratory. This is what I thought I'd get when I pursued weight loss. However, I ended up with a vicious cycle of survival-mode all-or-nothing insanity. Seeking approval and belonging through the desirability of body image demanded I threaten my access to food. Inevitably, as one survival need threatened a bigger more important survival need, my mind warped, ultimately presenting itself as a paranoia of food, obsessive body image, and eventually an eating disorder.

IMPORTANT: Each and every aspect of survival mode is wired
to preserve life. When looking at fear of body fat and food, clearly
what triggers these mechanisms go beyond being hunted by a
tiger and chased by a bear. These are dangers that aren't as easily

defined. But when danger in the end represents death, how people orient themselves in self-defense can sometimes be easier to see.

The difference between life and death is all-or-nothing. *If you fail, you will die.* For that reason, danger is felt with the same sharp dualistic risk. Thinking about danger tends to be black or white, this or that, right or wrong, and with little wiggle room for lenience or mistakes. This would make sense in situations where your ability to defend yourself from a predator, like a bear, demands you are precise in your decisions when choosing to fight, run away, or seek places to hide.

When it comes to how our minds work when we believe we are in a higher risk of danger, it would make sense that our self-defense would have the same black-and-white, unforgiving approach—even if real threat doesn't actually exist.

Perceived danger distorts the mind to see through a lens that interprets reality with all-or-nothing risk. Although, when you add self-awareness to the situation, an evaluation of one's capacity to defend and protect oneself makes threat a sliding scale that has room to move between all and nothing.

The more self-confident a person is under the circumstance, the less risk is felt, and the less perfectionistic they'd need to be. Therefore, I assume the more a person feels unsure, weak, and inadequate within themselves when facing threat, that he or she would be more perfectionistic or "all-or-nothing" with how they deal with it. You could say, survival mode changes how we experience and perceive the world around us, and this directs how we respond. One way to describe this is that we experience a change in consciousness.

The best description of consciousness with respect to survival mode I have read is from Sir David R. Hawkins, MD, PhD. (1927-2012) Similar to Maslow's

Hierarchy of Needs that correlates human motivation to fulfilling survival needs, Dr. Hawkins theorized a "map of consciousness" correlating human awareness and behavior based on levels of consciousness.

Chapter 3

The Lower States of Consciousness and Survival Mode

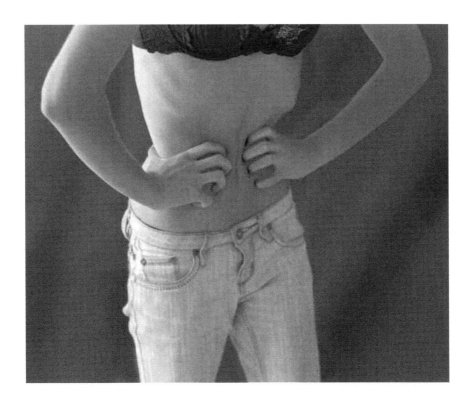

"When one realizes that one is the universe, complete and at one with all that is, forever without end, no further suffering is possible."

– Dr. David R. Hawkins, I, page xxii

Sir David R. Hawkins, MD., PhD, and His Map of Consciousness®

In my opinion, the best explanation and description of how our minds work in survival mode is from Sir David R. Hawkins, MD, PhD. This chapter focuses on what he describes as the lower states of consciousness. The higher levels of consciousness are applied in the discussion of recovery in the book, *Surrendering Your Survival.*

His research findings were published widely in medical, scientific, and psychoanalytic journals. For a complete history and biography of Dr. Hawkins, as well as information about the Map of Consciousness, go to this website at: www.veritaspub.com.

> **NOTE:** Dr. Hawkins' work has been of particular interest to me because he is the only person who has described in detail the process I went through in suicidal depression, the trap of suffering with an eating disorder, as well as the freedom I experienced in recovery. I have studied his work and watched countless hours of his lectures, getting to know the Map of Consciousness that he researched and published in 1995 his book, *Power vs. Force.* For copyright reasons, I cannot provide a picture of the Map of Consciousness or describe each individual level. This information is thoroughly depicted and described in *Power vs. Force* and other literature found at www.veritaspub.com.

The Map of Consciousness incorporates "stages" of spiritual evolution that Dr. Hawkins identified as levels of awareness that correspond to an energy level of life within a range from 0–1000. Unlike Maslow's hierarchy of needs observing survival-oriented motivation largely at the bottom and decreasing towards the pinnacle of the pyramid at the top, Dr. Hawkins' map addresses how survival mode blocks consciousness from the lowest, most limiting and primal stages of awareness (zero), working up to the most un-inhibited expanse of human enlightenment (1000).

He taught that with each progressive rise in consciousness there is an increase in the "frequency" or "vibration" of energy and awareness experienced.

> **NOTE:** *This chapter is focusing on the lower states of consciousness. I will address the higher states of consciousness in* Surrendering Your Survival *when I discuss recovery.*

Dr. Hawkins has described the lower stages of consciousness from 0–199 as elements of the narcissistic core of the ego that are self-serving and victim-oriented, and serve as the survival mechanisms of consciousness. This constricting, forceful, and negative self-centered consciousness was important and necessary for the evolution and survival of the species. However, it is also the source of fear, war, terror, and much suffering and psychological pain today and throughout history.

The positive levels of consciousness from 200–1000, are levels of independence, truth, and progressively have more acceptance, compassion and lovingness towards all of life, unconditional grace, as well as openness to reality.

> **NOTE:** The Map of Consciousness described by Dr. Hawkins is a specific understanding of human nature as it relates to perceptions of life, ourselves, others, and our world. As it concerns Dr. Abraham Maslow's Hierarchy of Needs, I see them both working in unison—one as an outline of what can trigger the survival mode, or the lower levels of consciousness, and the other explaining how we respond to those triggers, depending on the level of consciousness we are experiencing. Both describe the goal of transcending survival mode in order to move into higher

levels of human function. The Map of Consciousness describes the release from survival mode into nonduality and enlightenment, similar to Maslow's description of self-esteem and the progression into self-actualization.

The way I understand consciousness is that our thoughts, beliefs, motivations, and behaviors are predictable based on the level of consciousness we exist in. People that exist in shame typify the same thoughts and responses. The same goes for people in the inflated state of pride, and their predictable need to make others wrong. According to Dr. Hawkins, a person's way of being reflects the level of consciousness she's residing in.

On the next page is a chart I've put together describing how these lower states of survival think and feel, using the idea behind Dr. Hawkins' scale of consciousness.

Consciousness is impersonal as a person doesn't control or possess a level of awareness. It isn't theirs to claim. Rather, they experience a level of awareness that is available to all other people at that level, as a birthright.

For example, when a person says she is perfectionistic, she's identifying that symptom as a unique characteristic. However, that symptom stems from a level of consciousness that all people at that awareness and energy level would have. The same applies to selfishness, all-or-nothing thinking, empathy, courage, and forgiveness. These are qualities that typify different levels of consciousness and awareness, not the characteristics of the individual experiencing them. Like clouds blocking the sun's light and warmth, with more light there's more to see. It isn't a personal quality if you can or can't see, but rather a function of more or less light being accessible.

MODE	HOW THE MIND THINKS	HOW THE MIND FEELS
CAN HANDLE THREAT, FEAR OF LOSS — FIGHT TO DEFEND SUCCESS	I HAVE WHAT OTHERS WANT. / MY WAY OF LIFE IS BETTER THAN YOURS. / I'M BETTER THAN YOU. / LOSER'S ARE WORTHLESS. / I KNOW ALL THERE IS TO KNOW. / I'LL DO WHATEVER IS NECESSARY TO WIN.	**PRIDE (fighting to keep status)** Inflating self to be better than the factual truth, self-righteous, zealotry, "I'm right-you're wrong," scorns and stigmatizes others, positions one's self to be superior and valued above others.
FIGHT TO GAIN SUCCESS	I'M GOING TO GET WHAT I WANT. / LIFE WILL BE BETTER WHEN _____ (FILL IN THE BLANK). / THOSE PEOPLE HAVE WHAT I WANT. / IF ONLY WHAT I HAVE COULD BE BETTER.	**ANGER (fighting for gain)** Unrewarded desire, intitled to what's deserved, hate, vengeful, strength and aggression, threatens others, violence, frustration, justified in hurtful behavior. **DESIRE (wanting more)** Discontent with reality, insatiable wanting, craving, fantasizing, high energy and focus chasing ideals, trap of vanity and enslavement to it.

MODE	HOW THE MIND THINKS	HOW THE MIND FEELS
CANNOT HANDLE THREAT. COPING WITH LOSS — FREEZE, SHRINK, DISAPPEAR, "FIT IN"	I DON'T HAVE WHAT I WANT. / LIFE IS FEARFUL AND SCARY. / I AM ANXIOUS AND WORRIED ABOUT LOSS AND FAILURE. / LOSS AND FAILURE IS OUT THERE. / BE QUIET, BE LIKE EVERYONE ELSE, AND BLEND IN. / I'VE LOST WHAT I WANT.	**FEAR (fear of loss)** Anxiety, insecure, withdrawal, views life as hazardous, restless activity, procrastination. **GRIEF (loss)** Regret, disappointment, sadness, despondency, constant sense of loss. **APATHY (hopeless)** Despair, abdication, hopelessness, death through passive suicide.
FLIGHT, RUN AWAY, ISOLATION, HIDE	I DON'T DESERVE WHAT I WANT. / EVERYONE KNOWS I'M A FAILURE. / I'M WORTHY OF ABANDONMENT. / I AM HOPELESS. LIFE IS HOPELESS. / MY LIFE IS WORTHLESS.	**GUILT (blame others for loss)** Martyrdom, vindictive, victimhood, blame, destruction, suicidal threats. **SHAME (blame self for loss)** Scorn within self, misery, banishment, humiliation, cruelty to self and others.

HOW SURVIVAL MODES THINK AND FEEL

Lower States of Consciousness and Modes of Survival

In my mind, I visualize the lower levels of consciousness (which are survival-mode levels) in two halves. The lower half represents the freeze, flight, and hide response to perceived danger. The upper half represents the work, fight, and exaggeration in one's ability as a response to perceived vulnerability. What divides a person when presented with a threat is competence. If you don't have what it takes, your response is in fear and hiding. If you think you can get what it takes, you're going to work and fight for it. Keep in mind, whether you are on the side of fighting or the side of hiding, these survival states are based on the perception that you can't handle the danger without help from an action, substance, activity, or person. Fighting has help, hiding doesn't.

When You Can't Handle Threat

I've broken the inability to handle perceived danger into three parts: fear of loss, exposure, and abandonment.

The lowest levels of consciousness are based on exposed loss and failure, and above that is hiding from loss and failure. These lowest levels are founded on a sense of weakness and not feeling capable of handling threat, which promotes a predictable flight, shrink, and hide response to fear and vulnerability of danger. Additionally, as there's exposed loss in social status, perceived danger of abandonment and rejection goes up, which shifts motivation away from fighting for improved status towards fighting for basic survival needs, such as food.[24]

> **1) Fear of Loss (Freeze, Shrink, Disappear, or "Fit In")**
> Once it is perceived that "Alone I can't handle this, and I don't have help," if there is adequate energy, the reaction would be to do something, like hide, distract, or do something in fear.

- **Fear:** The energy of fear manifests in anxiety, restless energy, and perceptions that life is scary and dangerous. At this level you are likely to withdraw and hide from exposure, cower away, blend in, or "shrink" like animals that attempt to remove themselves, and run from threat.

2) Exposure and Loss (Flight, Run and Hide)

Being exposed to threat and losing can feel *as if you've lost the source of your happiness.* In eating disorders, that loss would be loss of being thinner, or the loss of being able to eat. Some people get stuck in paralysis in grief as the exposure and loss feels permanent and defining.

- **Grief:** In grief there is energy to cope with loss by repressing it, going into denial, avoidance, anger, and continued hiding. Because of this denial, there is also depression, avoiding the truth in anticipation of not being able to handle the loss. In grief there is enough energy to express sadness, regret, and victimhood, and when the energy to express these emotions is too much, people can go into apathy.

- **Apathy:** At apathy there isn't enough energy to deny and repress. Instead there is despair and hopelessness. It feels as if there is permanent loss to happiness. The common thought is that you might as well give up everything. In this space, there is no energy for effort, and life feels meaningless. Passive suicide, like refusal to eat or refusing medical treatment, occurs when people exist at this level of victimhood.

3) Abandonment and Rejection (Isolation)

At these lowest levels of consciousness, it is perceived that loss is unrecoverable, and is defining a person as "bad." It is a dangerous level as energy is devoted to damaging oneself and others as it is believed that irreparable damage has been done.

- **Guilt:** Guilt is a last-ditch victim-and-martyr defense mechanism. Holding oneself and others to a concept of what things should be, and accusing all non-adherence as sinful and inadequate. With guilt, people are still willing to seek approval, bargain, and work to regain approval.[25] Although, they are filled with resentment, pessimism, fault-finding, and can be destructive with themselves and others in their desperation to make things better.

- **Shame:** The lowest state of consciousness is shame, when a person internalizes failure and loss as an indication of her personal inferiority, unlovability, and inadequacy. She lives with internalized stigma, humiliation, and banishes herself from others. Shame is often accompanied by a sense of shrinking or being small, and by a sense of exposure in front of a real or imagined audience.[26] People in shame have a heightened sense of needing to repair themselves, and are highly sensitive to opinions, both positive and negative.[25]

According to evolutionary psychology:

- Shame is an intense survival-mode trigger to fend for oneself as stigma and shunning elicits the sense you have no social value and will be alone—having to fend for your own survival needs in order to sustain life.[24]

- Shame is linked to fighting for personal survival by seeking what will make her feel better, without reliance on others. Drugs, alcohol, medication, but especially food, has been seen as a way to self-soothe, or to preserve one's own sense of survivability.[27]

— Shame, and the loss of social status, enhances the value of Maslow's first and second hierarchies of need. The value of food goes up significantly as more shame is experienced.[24]

— People living in chronic shame often experience paranoia, delusions, and psychosis, and are cruel to themselves, animals, and to life around them.[28] "If I can't have, no one can." Life is evil. Suicidal behaviors are common.

MY EXPERIENCE: *From my personal experience suffering with an eating disorder, I recognize each and every lower level of consciousness. At the bottom of shame, not only did I fixate on controlling the organization and cleanliness of my home (the second hierarchy of need), but I also fixated on controlling food and my body, ultimately experiencing massive swings between starving myself and bingeing episodes (the first hierarchy of need).*

As I believed my social status in my family's religion and with God couldn't be repaired, I shifted my focus towards my own sense of status by using body image. Unfortunately, this choice threatened my basic security with food, promoting fear of food, and abandonment associated to weight gain. Ultimately, it felt like I would be rejected, alone, and in misery forever if I couldn't maintain a safe balance between eating, starving, and maintaining my façade of thinness.

The consciousness level of "Fear," I felt anxious, insecure, and in the level of "Guilt," I felt desperate with continuous impulsivity to do something immediately. Much of the purging behavior came out of the "Guilt" level of consciousness. And when I felt I had failed the diet, "Shame" associated with failure definitely triggered massive food binges. I also recall the higher levels of lower consciousness. This is the fighting aspect of survival mode.

When You Can Handle Threat

The other half of survival mode is based on fighting against fear. It is more energized and more confident in believing something can be done. When there is a perceived threat, there is a sense that "with assistance, or with a weapon, I can handle it." However, the underlying belief is that without aid, one cannot handle threat alone, which is ultimately why a situation triggers a "threat" response in the first place.

- The major dividing factor between the lower flight or hiding response and the upper fighting response is the illusion that by having an external weapon, or help, a person perceives she can handle it. She thinks she can take on the threat—*like thinking you'll be more confident if you are thinner.*

- Unfortunately, this confidence relies on getting something or acquiring something outside of one's truthful sense of ability—*like having to diet and restrict food to get and keep the thinner body.*

- This means that whatever sense of capacity a person thinks she has, it's coming from the attachment to her weapon and not from her innate capacity to handle it— like only feeling confident to socialize if you are thinner.

- Therefore, although she feels a sense of capacity, that confidence is inflated because of the conditions—*like thinking you are superior at a social event because you are the thinnest person there.*

- However, because it isn't true internal capacity, the confidence is conditional, ultimately making this level of consciousness very controlling, fearful, and vulnerable to losing those conditions—*like feeling inferior and deflated because someone else is thinner than you at a social event.*

Fighting

This half of survival mode is based on striving, wanting, getting, posturing, and promoting oneself. It is boastful, self-inflating, and also more manipulative and controlling. Similar to the descriptions of narcissism, this level of survival mode attempts to stigmatize and criticize others in order to gain security with superiority and power. It starts with a sense of confidence and capacity to get what is needed. This conditional and dependent sense of ability to handle perceived danger is broken into three parts: desire, anger, and pride.

- **Desire:** Above fear and the perception of threat is a sense that with hard work and acquiring certain things and conditions, a sense of capacity, safety, and success can be gained. At the level of desire is a hopeful yearningness for obtaining the conditions that provide an outer sense of strength. "I will feel better when (fill in the blank)" is a common thought.

  Desire is energized by the fantasy that by getting what is needed, life will be free from fear. This is like finding a weapon in the wilderness. Consciousness at this level is associated with cravings, longings, fantasizing, and perfectionism. It is highly productive and energized by the illusion that permanent confidence and security is within reach when certain conditions are met. Unfortunately, because desire comes out of a sense of inherent inadequacy, and reaches outside of one's nature to fulfill a conditional form of security, it is a trap of continuous seeking, wanting, yearning, and striving. Even as a goal is accomplished or acquired, there is never the satisfaction she thought she'd get.

Like the expense of chasing a mirage, the internal sense of inadequacy still exists because safety is dependent on continuous outside, extrinsic acquisition. The acquirement is a form of bondage, withholding freedom of true self-esteem, in exchange for the estate of "when I reach the goal."

The entire weight-loss and beauty industry is based on the consciousness of desire: *If you restrict food properly and exercise hard enough, you can make the body thinner, and you too can feel safe from the threat of abandonment.*

- **Anger:** As desire commands incredible feats of energy, work, and focus, without reward comes the resentment and frustration of victimhood. This level of consciousness has enough perceived strength (with certain conditions or "weapons") to make threats and demands using the high energy of anger. Much oppression has been liberated from accessing the confidence and energy of this level.

Rage is used to demand and force rewards to which the work of desire feels entitled. It stems from a sense of unfairness as life energy has been spent, and promised rewards weren't achieved. There is hate, jealously, aggression, and violence.

This reminds me of times when I felt that I deserved weight loss after expending thousands of calories through exercise, and suffering through intense hunger in order to adhere to precise restrictions of food. Ultimately, this resentment and anger resulted in justified overeating that always ended in binge-eating episodes. *Food became the reward to compensate me for unrewarded desire for weight loss.*

- **Pride:** At the top of survival mode is the prideful, superior, inflated idea of one's ability to defeat others and defend herself. Like the rest of the lower states of consciousness, pride is still weak and dependent on outside acquirement and conditions. With pride, as the conditions are acquired and met, an internalization or self-attachment to the accomplishment (as if it is a truthful representation of internal capacity) inflates one's sense of her ability to be bigger than it truthfully is. Achievements are displayed, discussed, and made to be the focus of attention. I believe this is why people like to post pictures/selfies of their thinner and fitter body, as a display of success. Or why some women magnify, draw attention to, and accentuate certain body parts, as if they literally inflated these parts like a balloon, like her eyelashes, lips, breasts, and butt.

She thinks, "I have what is desired, therefore I am successful, superior, and safe." Because, underneath it all, she feels weak and insecure independent of those conditions, and she overcompensates desired success to display a superficial signal of competence. This is similar to a threatened animal that feels insecure, and thus expands itself to promote the illusion of being larger.

I visualize this as someone in full armor, holding every weapon imaginable, and professing that he is the strongest person in the world. When in reality, despite all of his attainments, inside the armor is the truth of a person, who without protection might actually be too weak and incapable of handling it. This is like the narcissistic anorexic believing she is safe and successful in her thinness, as a symbol of superior capacity to restrain herself, even though the truth is she has to isolate herself from life, is lethargic and paranoid, and has insecurity around others who are more emaciated than she.

Request for my help from a woman in her 40's:
Hi Robin, to be honest, I wouldn't be contacting you if it weren't for my friend. I feel there really is no hope and what can you tell me that I already don't know. But right now, I'm struggling a lot. I'm 43, mom of four, had eating disorders all my life and have seen a host of different people about it. Also, I've had past drug abuse and went to outpatient rehab for that. Eating disorders are the very worst for me though.

Unlike a lot of other eating disorder sufferers, I could present to you who I am and the nature of my disease within five minutes of talking to you. I've seen every therapist in the book and did 6.5 years in Overeaters Anonymous in my mid-to-late 20s. I know what my issues are, but I just don't know how I'm supposed to stop.

The Upside and Downside of Pride

Because pride is based in desire, it is also insatiable and demands continuous achievement. This also makes pride competitive, encourages comparison to others, and the deflation of others, in order to attain the ultimate goal of supremacy. This desire for betterment and power over others promotes a need to be right and to make others wrong.

This is the primary narcissistic reasoning behind stigma—to blame others for problems, deflect weakness away from oneself and towards others—with the goal to exploit and keep others down, in order to acquire and maintain power.

The downside of the pride level of consciousness is that because it is based on a lie presenting a better and superior persona, if it is exposed, and the power of superiority is lost to inferiority, and the natural consequence is a plummet down to the lowest state of consciousness: shame.

Many of the women I've worked have greater shame about gaining weight—because at one point in their life they took pride in their thinness. Because they attached superiority to the conditions of their thinner body, as their weight naturally increased because of pregnancy, age, injury, or stress of life, they experienced a descent in consciousness that left them in hiding, in guilt and embarrassment, and exposed in shame. I know for me, I was trapped inside the pride of the conditions of my "perfected" body that I would rather commit suicide than to fail and gain weight.

Pride is the source of self-righteousness, religious and political zealotry, and radicalism used to justify war, conquering, and oppression of others. Pride and shame could be considered the most radical, and potentially the most destructive survival modes of consciousness.

IMPORTANT: The entire spectrum of lower consciousness functions as important survival mechanisms. Without these fight-or-flight impulses, the human species wouldn't exist today, especially as it concerns the foundational hierarchies of needs, such as food, shelter, and safety.

And if our lives weren't positively affected by loving relationships, these mechanisms wouldn't be so sensitive to our interactions with others, and how we are perceived.

As much as lower levels of consciousness are an aspect of survival, they are ultimately a source of pain, anguish, and suffering for many people.

When it comes to radical fears and resultant coping mechanisms, like eating disorders, people suffering in this state of mind aren't looking at things realistically. Their perceptions of danger are extreme, which means their responding self-defense is extreme too. As a result, their survival mechanisms are approached in an unforgiving and all-or-nothing perfectionistic way, as if it's life or death.

These mechanisms and how fear manifest psychologically, are best described as *cognitive distortions*. This is how our mind thinks and functions when apparent threat distorts how we perceive, process, and respond to our environment. Unfortunately, with distorted perceptions that make it seem as if perfectionistic thinking is safe, ideals are set that are unrealistic and unforgiving. These self-oriented distortions are described by Dr. Hawkins *as the narcissistic core of the ego.* This ego is where body image goes beyond the need to "fit in" to functioning as a way to be seen as superior than other.

When the body image portrayed for people to aspire to is a sanctimonious image of arrogance and elitism, it's no wonder the goal rises as people reach it. In narcissistic cultures, it would be predictable then that followers would suffer from more intense symptoms of exaggerated narcissism. This is particularly true when looking at narcissistic body-image concepts of thin(ner) and health(ier) supremacy.

Email seeking my help from 26-year-old woman:

…Unless I'm not thin enough by "my standards"—flat stomach, tanned, toned, no cellulite at all, etc.—I don't think I'm feminine. When I'm not thin, I equate myself as repulsive, masculine, hairy, and unattractive, as the comments from men have continued to affect me over the years.

My dad made fun of my short-bitten fingernails and said how disgusting they were. Because of this I've spent tens of thousands of dollars on acrylic fingernails over the past 10 years to maintain nice long fingernails like a "female." I'm too ashamed for a guy to ever see my short fingernails. Once when I didn't have time to get my nails done before going out on a date with a guy I panicked and put band-aids on each of my fingers so he didn't have to see them.

My grandpa told me my lip was hairy, and there were two boys who were my next-door neighbors who made fun of me for having upper lip hair and a deep male voice. I remember shaving my entire body after my grandpa told me I was hairy. Today, when I go out with guys, I compulsively make sure there is not one single hair on my body (I used to wax my face).

When I know I'm going out with a man, I don't eat on the day I go out with them. I exercise. I buy a new outfit. I get my nails done. I even put on a higher-pitched voice just for him, so he doesn't think I sound masculine. It's crazy looking back at what I have done for a guy, but my body is literally in a chronic state of fight or flight now for most of my life around men, and I would rather (in my head at least) fail college another 10 times than be rejected by a man.

———————————————————

"The thought 'I can only be happy if I win or get what I want' is a guarantee of worry, anxiety, and unhappiness."

– Dr. David R. Hawkins

SECTION 2

Surviving in a Narcissistic Culture

"Until you make the unconscious conscious, it will direct your life and you will call it fate."

– Carl Jung

Chapter 4

Narcissistic Survival Mode

"Not everything that is faced can be changed. But nothing can be changed until it is faced."

– James Baldwin

NOTE: The topic of narcissism has been studied and discussed for decades. In recent years there's been increased dialogue concerning the victims of narcissistic abuse, especially since these victims are the people willing to reach out for psychological help. Due to the complexity of this topic, and the fact that I am not an expert, I will discuss only what I believe is relevant to the topic of body image and its influence in eating disorders.

In this chapter, I will discuss narcissism from a simple point of view. In the next chapter (5), I will look at body image and eating disorders through the lens of narcissism to make better sense of how and why these beliefs and behaviors function. Before discussing narcissism as it relates to eating disorders, I believe it's important to understand how it functions in all of us, particularly when the culture that we are seeking love and approval from encourages a grandiose version of it. Helping people takes a gentle and compassionate approach when guiding them to be able to see the narcissism that's driving the pride and shame they feel about their body.

When looking at narcissism as part of human nature, it helps people understand their own behavior without needing to hide, repress, or be embarrassed by it.

Most people take offense and become defensive when they hear themselves associated with narcissism because they've always linked the word to extremely self-centered and sometimes horribly abusive and malicious people. But in order to understand recovery, it's imperative a person recognize the narcissistic drive behind the toxic emotions attached to her body that project a distorted fear onto food. If I can get a person to see the symbolism of thin(ner)-supremacy concepts that she's defined her body by as narcissistic, she might have space to see with clarity that her relationship with food is dysfunctional as a result.

Narcissism: Being Special is Being Loved

When thinking about narcissism, a simple way to understand it is this: *it's a desire to be and feel special*—which often encourages you to stand out positively when compared to others.

The sense is that by upholding concepts that are promoted as "special," you will be seen as important—and that will diminish the risk of being left out by the group of people where you are seeking to be included.

This need for being seen as extraordinary promotes effort to uniquely shine and have the spotlight as a way to earn security in a group and to defend oneself from exclusion. To narcissism, being "special" means you have value and worth as a person.

On some level, each and every one of us is hardwired with narcissism. It is a self-preserving survival mechanism that functions to create an allure of "importance" about you, so that others will want and need you. Think of this desire for specialness as a defense mechanism wired to fulfill Maslow's third hierarchy of survival needs, particularly when your value is defined in comparison to others.

When the family and culture you live in worships and makes a body image of thinness "special," it would make sense that people who are seeking to promote and defend themselves from exclusion would yearn to be thinner. Being thinner in this type of environment signifies that you're exceptional and have qualities that make a better human being. Some of the people that I've helped, describe that by being thinner, their family will look up to them, will be proud and put them on a pedestal of success. They think that this success will be so defining that it is the key to earn the right and privilege of living life freely, without having to defend their success. These fantasies stem from inner narcissism that desires and seeks to have earned proof of one's worth and right to inclusion.

When Narcissism is Beneficial

To varying degrees, narcissism and the desire to feel special is normal and healthy, especially when growing up and learning how to assimilate into one's family and culture. Any person would want her family and friends to believe she "fits in"—and is an important contributing member who has value and worth. Again, being "special" equates to being lovable.

Our human desire to be seen positively by important people in our life promotes a space of higher energy and encourages effort that goes beyond our natural tendencies. It ignites a willingness to work hard, despite weaknesses, and to learn and grow, which is essential when developing a sense of capacity. The benefit of this desire to impress family, teachers, and friends is that it can energize and extrinsically motivate you to follow the rules, do what you're told, and do a good job at it.

> **It could be argued that narcissism is an important motivational component when learning to adapt to societal norms, which ultimately ends up promoting the development of self-awareness, competence, and independence to be one's true self.**

For this eventual self-awareness to become apparent, at some point a person must recognize the distinct differences between her true self and the conceptual idea of who her family and culture wants her to be. To do this, you must have the courage to face criticism and possible rejection by exposing the truth of your inadequacies, when instincts and cognitive dissonance direct you to do otherwise.

To narcissism, lying shields us from the vulnerable truth,

and in this state of mind we are wired to cope by shrinking, hiding, denying, or deflecting anything that exposes our weakness.

Admitting flaws is very difficult when it threatens your status, "specialness," or earning others' approval, but it's inevitable that mistakes will be made when learning and striving to achieve goals or meet demands with the intent to impress family—more so when the ideals and goals that we are held to are out of touch with human nature and reality. It would seem safer to lie and hide your true self. However, when important people, like parents and teachers, provide a forgiving environment that gives a person grace for her errors, even when others perform better, there is safety for her to be truthful about perceived faults without being defined as less worthy of love and inclusion.

How Humility Effects Narcissism

A safe space with family and friends where a child can be truthful when she's vulnerable to criticism is fundamental to cultivate humility. Humility allows a person to express the honesty of his integrity and expose the truth of his faults, without being defined as "bad." With this grace, children learn that being "special" doesn't mean you have to be perfect, the best, or better than others, in order to be accepted and worthy of love. It also means you don't have to strictly internalize cultural ideology that you don't naturally align with, in order to be worthy of love.

According to Dr. Kristin Neff, an author and psychologist from the University of Texas, self-esteem is an inner evaluation about how valuable a person is: very valuable, not so good, not valuable at all.[6] This is different than self-compassion, which isn't about self-evaluation at all, but rather about being kind to oneself. According to Dr. Neff,

> *"Self-compassion is a healthy source of self-worth because it's not contingent and it's unconditional. It's much more stable over time*

because it is not dependent on external markers of success such as grades."

A humble approach to mistakes and successes is essential when transcending narcissism to develop a sense of self-compassion that is true and real, and based on inherent competency. Ultimately, this teaches a person to hold inner grace for herself, and it allows her to be self-directed and realistic about her capacity, risks, and goals, even as others around her are more advanced. *A person with this type of self-awareness is less likely to internalize "specialness" as what makes her life important.* So, when she makes mistakes, is inadequate, or inferior when compared to others, her life doesn't lose meaning or value.

People who are raised to earn approval with the arrogance of narcissism to be superior or the best, suffer with the consequence of anxiety and stress when being compared to others, and when they underperform, they shrink in shame and self-pity as their results are used to define their worthlessness. With self-compassion, you're given the grace to be truthful about yourself and your human condition, without being defined as being superior or inferior.[6]

Even when a person is rejected and disapproved of, especially when expectations are attached to ideals that are clearly unrealistic, with self-awareness and self-compassion the goal is seen as inappropriate or flawed—not the intrinsic worth of the person being held to it. With compassion, fear about criticism goes away and a person can have the discernment and humility to recognize and admit her true capacity, which makes glorified superficial ideals and concepts less important. In this case, being "special" loses its appeal, especially when it's attached to inappropriate expectations that require suffering and unrealistic perfectionism.

Still, if she is capable of reaching the glorified standards, and is more successful at meeting challenges, this humility recognizes *the lie of arrogant*

*narcissism—which is that this makes her more special or her life more impor-
tant than others.* Another way to describe arrogant narcissism is when someone becomes narcissistic, meaning the way she feels special is to be superior
to others.

When Narcissism Becomes Narcissistic

When a person is narcissistic, she can't afford to be humble or realistic because that would mean she's "normal," and normal is inferior. The survival
drive and desire to be the center of attention, and also viewed as important,
sets a person up to inflate or exaggerate her worth, which doesn't allow for
truthfulness, self-compassion, or humility.

There's an increased need to lie about a person's true capacity in order to
promote herself, particularly when others seem to have more success or
more of the spotlight. Without humility, being special doesn't include the
grace for mistakes or the truth, and when another person has more success
and gets more attention, that can seem threatening to a person trying to
survive with unforgiving arrogant narcissism. If she thinks she is losing importance to the people who give her the spotlight, her natural response
would be to belittle anybody she thinks is competition, done as a way to
steal the spotlight and to convince others to ignore the other person.

> **The need to lie and to make oneself seem superior to others
> could be argued as a narcissistic survival mechanism that de-
> velops when a person hasn't experienced 1) the grace of self-
> compassion and 2) the humility it takes to admit relative
> inadequacy.**

With humility, the entire concept of supremacy changes because success
and being better at something than another person *is seen as relative.* A person with humility wouldn't internalize her successes as a symbol of superiority over others because her gifts, talents, and goals in life aren't directed

by how she compares to others. Humility makes this comparison as a way to define someone's intrinsic worth seem nonsensical, especially if that spotlight of success demands unrealistic conditions and expectations for others to achieve.

To truthful people, superiority is irrelevant because there's value given to working in reality over trying to force a fantasy. Truth allows for a natural process necessary for individuals to grow and evolve from within themselves, which allows for them to intrinsically define what brings their life strength and joy. It would be easier to be real and true, and accept narcissistic judgment and criticism, than to have to perform above and beyond one's capacity to maintain a false front so that others approve of your supremacy.

The willingness to let go of approval that's attached to superior "specialness" that requires perfectionism and comparison to others, gives a person independence to validate herself and to be truthful about who she is. This opens the mind to get beyond narcissism and needing others' approval to feel worthy of inclusion. The space of truth transcends the self-oriented defensiveness of survival mode to access a higher level of consciousness in order to take the risks and reap the rewards of being self-directed, curious, and free to explore life. Yet, when you're raised in a family and culture that encourages narcissistic thinking, and that demeans and judges anything different, allowing yourself to be real and truthful would seem dangerous. It would be safer to reject your truth to pursue concepts of supremacy and to strive to be better than you actually are.

The more a person abandons herself to chase a narcissistic mirage of inclusion, the more she'll need attention, approval, and validation to supply a sense of success. This would entail that she hold herself to a superior standard that defines success. These standards typically come from narcissistic cultures and ideologies that seek superiority, or to be "the best."

When You're Raised in a Narcissistic Culture

In some groups and cultures, being "the best" or superior is how a person identifies herself as "special." These cultures are narcissistic and have narcissistic belief systems that are driven with idealism as a way to define the worth of a person's life.

In these groups, the drive of narcissism to be special goes beyond the desire to be included. The goal is to dominate, control, and to be seen as the authority.

The illusion is that by being the authority, you can control everything and won't be vulnerable to exclusion and abandonment.

These narcissistic cultures typically are the source of dogma. They are the "sacred authority" that is to be followed and to never be questioned. They hold the power to define 1) who you are, 2) what you stand for, and 3) what you are to do with your life. These cultures present themselves as superior, but they are controlling, forceful, fear-based, and perfectionistic—and there is no grace for mistakes and no humility to be truthful.

I've come to observe that the majority of people suffering from eating disorders (including my own experience with it), are suffering from trying to fulfill their third hierarchy of need with a narcissistic belief system. They are in "narcissistic survival mode" trying to conform to and be accepted by a belief system that is only inclusive when ideals are perfectly and dogmatically conformed to.

Based on inherent survival mechanisms, we're all hardwired to be defensive to perceptions of inadequacy, as well as the vulnerly of being rejected. However, a person having attached his or her life-security to a belief of supremacy, would

experience a more sensitive trigger to being narcissistic as a defense mechanism.

One way to think about someone who's in *"narcissistic survival mode"* is that he or she is "addicted" to, or dependent on feeling authoritatively special, just to feel safe. This makes sense when in order to survive, a person wants to be included and accepted into a culture that is narcissistic.

In order to belong, he identifies who he is from a fantasy of being notably superior to others, because this means he will be loved and accepted. To feel good, he can't just be himself. He has to be a concept of something better, and that must be "the best," in contrast to others. Otherwise he'd experience "withdrawals," like any addict. If feeling loved and included entails strict adherence and perfectionism in order to be superior, his mistakes or competition would be a source of danger and threat. Lying about the truth becomes "a way of being" in order to survive.

Email seeking my help from a woman in her early 40's:
Hi Robin, I started dieting when I was 13. I saved the money I earned from lawn mowing to buy diet pills I saw in a magazine. That is how the madness began. But my emotional issues and self-hatred were firmly rooted by then. I have an older sister, and she was perfect in my family's eyes, because she was skinny. She was seen as "special" and I was just average. Although, I was referred to as "fatty."

I was always compared negatively with my skinny sister, and I was consistently told to stop eating and asked why I couldn't look and behave more like her. This really pissed me off and I chose to rebel. I tried to be as different as possible and to stand out. I didn't realize how much more emotional damage I was doing to myself and what became years of yo-yo dieting, food obsession, and bingeing and dieting. I associated love and acceptance and beauty with having the perfect slim body. That was my goal in life: To be loved—and fixing my body was my way to get it. When I lost weight, I was admired, and when I gained weight, I was made fun of or ignored.

I have been on every diet…and each of them multiple times. I have starved myself and exercised three times a day, popping diet pills, and tried supplement after supplement. I'd tell myself, "This time will be different." Ya right. And after each failed attempt to maintain my weight loss I would feel less of a person, but I would always self-sabotage. Food was both my best friend and worst enemy.

At my highest I weighted 275 lbs., and at my lowest, 150 lbs. I must have lost and regained 1,000 lbs. over my dieting lifespan. It sickens me how much energy and time I've spent studying the latest diet fads, reading nutrition and exercise books, not to mention all the money I dished out. I see now I should have been in counseling and reading self-worth books.

The problem is: I don't know how to let go of my desire to be thinner, and I don't see how anyone could allow herself to feel like a failure or a loser? I simply don't see any way out. If I quit trying to be thinner, that's like quitting at trying to feel good about myself, or quitting at wanting to be loved. That seems cruel to me even when I know continuing to diet is just as cruel, and I'll end up bingeing anyways. How does one accept being obese when it feels like your life is worthless?

When Inclusion Requires You Conform to Narcissistic Beliefs

When parents believe narcissistic ideology without questioning it, it would make sense that they'd raise their children to believe and adhere to it the same way. Any parent who lives in radical fear of inferiority, predictability will raise his or her children to also seek superiority, thinking it will keep them safe from judgement. It would seem "loving" and like good parenting to dogmatically promote perfectionistic cultural ideals, and to expect your child to seek to be "the best." *For people functioning in narcissistic survival mode, teaching and promoting concepts of supremacy is a way to teach your children how to advance in life and be seen as worthy of love.*

But when parents promote narcissistic supremacy:

- They are inadvertently teaching their child that her natural capacity is inadequate, and that she should reject her truthful aptitude to instead inflate ideas of what her competency should be.

- As narcissistic-supremacy ideals are admired, children are encouraged to repress their genuine self to become a fake and seemingly stronger alternative.

- Their child is unconsciously taught to inhibit the truth in order to get praise and attention that supports what's expected.

- In cultures of narcissistic supremacy, a person's worth, value, and lovability are defined by her willingness to conform herself to cultural ideologies.

- In essence, their child represses her true identity to survive with a seemingly more lovable, but fake persona, or "fake self."

- Their child's identity changes to become a conceptualized lie as their true self is deemed inadequate or even dangerous, especially when compared to others who seem more superior.

- You are loved only when you become what your parents want you to be, and if someone is better at it than you, it can seem as if you still aren't good enough.

In narcissistic cultures, children are encouraged to lose touch with their authentic self, and to gain touch with the illusion of strength and safety that is attached to idealistic concepts of supremacy.

When your worth is measured by your willingness to strictly conform to perfectionistic ideals, it would make sense that you'd be compared in contrast to others who meet those ideals, as if they are modeling for you what to strive for.

For example:

- If your family believes in thin(ner) supremacy, and you have a sibling who is thinner than you, you will be defined as inferior to her, even if you are thin.

- If your family bases worth on school grades, a child who struggles to learn will be compared to someone else that has better grades.

- This makes it so that your worth is not only defined by the ideals you're held to, but also by how you rank compared to others who are also held to those standards.

The truth is, as a person strives to be superior with the intent to "survive," she instantly becomes relatively inferior to the goal and to others who seem to have more success. This raises the already-high standards, and makes past success seem inadequate. Unfortunately, because these concepts of supremacy are coming from fantasies that don't include normal human functioning, reaching the standards become more and more unrealistic and unachievable, and for most people, success at this level requires abnormal degrees of obsession, isolation from reality, and unforgiving perfectionism.

An example of this is thin supremacy—and the obsessive and compulsive anorexic behaviors as a result.

The standards of supremacy become so grandiose and totalitarian that they require of dogmatic believers a high degree of obsession, perfectionism, and isolation from life in order to succeed. However, most people fail to reach them, and instead of questioning the radicalism of the standard or the entire concept of narcissistic supremacy, people internalize that *they are flawed when they fail.* This is like how people who fail to perfectly restrict bad food in hopes to lose weight, binge in shame, and hide in embarrassment. The more safety a person attaches to narcissistic concepts of inclusion, the more likely she is to think her natural self is unsafe.

Narcissistic Survival Mode—It's All About "Comparison"

In relation to the ideals, no matter how much you devote your life to reaching them, if you're inferior in comparison to others, this translates to loss, embarrassment, disapproval, and abandonment. This positions a person's third hierarchy of need to demand that she stay in the spotlight, and always be "better than" and in control of how she's compared to others in order to feel safe. To defend her survival needs to belong and be included, she must fight and put others down to prove she's the best—as if being inadequate or inferior is like a "tiger" threatening her life. She'll do whatever is necessary to avoid being exposed as inadequate, as if it's a death threat. *This type of comparison is common in the narcissistic culture of thin(ner) supremacy.*

People suffering from anorexia can be highly competitive with each other, ranking girls based on their thinness, protruding bones, and thigh gaps that require radical starvation to achieve. Similarly, I've talked with countless women that are binge eaters who try to find others who are larger than them as a way to temporarily reduce feelings of failure and shame.

> **NOTE:** Many of the people I work with have described how they often compare their size and shape to others at an event. Many women suffering with an eating disorder tell me that when she compares herself to others attending the same event, if she is the thinnest person there, feelings of euphoria and elation come over her. But if someone else is more successful at matching the "ideal image," she internalizes this as a personal failure and will shrink in shame and embarrassment. She makes the assumption that everyone else at the event are grading the women based on who's the thinnest and who's the fattest. Being seen as inferior to someone else can ruin the entire experience for people who think this way.

This would be expected when being raised to be "the best." Growing up in this type of strict environment where you are constantly being compared to others, a child can't afford to be truthful about himself or his mistakes, especially when disappointment, guilt, and shame are used to encourage doing what you're told.

> **In a narcissistic culture, people are put in a position where they must be attached to something that others will approve of—which is called *narcissistic supply*. In this case, you must have something of superior status that compares better than others, in order to survive.**

Surviving with Narcissistic Supply

As much as narcissism can be a positive source of energy and willfulness to learn and work hard, it can be harmful when being "special" doesn't allow a child the safety to be his true authentic self, or the grace to make mistakes. When threats of punishment, criticism, and disappointment are used to motivate conformity in order to be accepted, a person isn't given a safe space to learn humility. *She isn't given the experience to learn that vulnerability, failures, and mistakes don't have to be shameful and defining.*

When you're taught that being lovable requires you to rigidly conform to concepts that others believe are "special," a child loses touch with her true self as she pursues inclusion based on emulating these concepts. Her motivation to be loved and accepted is directed toward becoming these concepts of superiority, rather than being directed toward expanding the truth of her authentic self. And when she fails and believes she is an irreparably damaged human being, instead of questioning the narcissistic belief system, she is likely to compensate or find a new "supply" in order to be seen as special and worthy of inclusion.

> **Narcissistic supply is any source of perceived superiority a person can attach herself to when compared to others. You could say that in a culture promoting narcissistic ideologies, that thin(ner) supremacy is just one source of many belief systems throughout time, selling and supplying a means to inclusion through supremacy.**

In our culture, being superior or "special" at being the life of the party, smart, athletic, wealthy, musically talented, religious, or materialistic, are just some of the sources that supply "specialness" to a narcissist.

When a person fails at being the best with one ideal, it would make sense that she needs to compensate by seeking to be the best at a different narcissistic ideal.

They are striving to stick out and to be viewed as having something special as if without that allure, you'd be left out, forgotten, and become vulnerable to being seen as inferior. Many of the people I've worked with felt that they were failures in some way because they didn't feel they had anything special, and to feel better about it, they focused their energy on trying to control their success at becoming thinner.

For clients that failed at being thin enough, they focused their energy on trying to succeed in academics, business, or being liked because they are funny.

For some people, the narcissistic supply they hold themselves to is not only providing a personal sense of worthiness, but it also supplies some extrinsic benefit to a person(s) giving her worth for that reason.

> **EXAMPLE:** I've had clients whose spouse not only demanded she rigidly restrict food so that she maintain a level of thinness that sexually aroused him, but he put her body under the spotlight in social situations as to magnify her sexually attractiveness for others to see. She was treated like his claimed property, as if she represented an extension of his superiority. She acted as "narcissistic supply" for her spouse who demanded she diet in order to look a certain way for his narcissistic benefit.

> Similarly, I've had clients whose parents fixated on the dangers of "unhealthy" food, and shamed "bad" food with religious vigor. As children, they hid food, binged when they were at friends' houses where they were free to eat forbidden food without judgment. These clients describe having to live a very restrictive lifestyle because they'd get in trouble and be shamed if they don't eat "healthy."

> Children, especially girls, learn early that ideas about the body matter, and that other people's opinion can determine how they

are treated. In cultures and families that promote narcissistic body images of beauty to their daughters, it's observed that "pretty" girls get more attention and, ultimately, are taught they can control their "status" and how they are perceived. Girls and women can become preoccupied with their own physical appearance as a way of anticipating and controlling how they are treated. This is an effect called "self-objectification," which is when a person perceives his or her body as an object that exists for the pleasure of others.[7] Basically, to gain inclusion and a sense of value a person might use his or her body as a tool of gratification for someone else's pleasure. Self-objectification with thinner ideals, increases a person's risks of disordered eating.[8]

I assume mental health issues would rise when there's self-objectification through any body image ideal, like supremacy beliefs about sexual purity and abstinence, and health supremacy with fear-based food restrictions. You are essentially doing with your body, what someone else demands you do, in fear of disappointing them and with the goal that they'll approve of you. It's as if they claim your body as their own, and you've given it to them thinking they'll love you in return.

Many people have described to me how they had a parent who was obsessed with his/her own fatness and thinness. This parent made size, weight, and thinness a central topic when discussing their own and other people's body. This emphasis on thinness came with equal fixation on "fattening" or bad food, and typically their children were encouraged to diet at a very young age. As you would expect, some of these children responded by conforming to the goal to be thinner, but in many cases they responded by sneaking and wanting the food that was restricted, and by overeating when that food was available.

As children in this position eventually gain more and more weight, their thin(ner)-supremist parents become more and more embarrassed and concerned that their child's growing size will be shamed, the same way they shame others who are larger.

Like the thinner child being praised and promoted in public, the fatter child is hidden and pressured to diet in order to lose weight.

When thinness or concepts of healthiness are supplying the parents with narcissistic supremacy, it would make sense that they would want the same for their children. Unfortunately, a child raised in this type of environment isn't exposed to what it's like *to be valued unconditionally.*

One of the most consistent symptoms described by all the people I've worked with who suffer with some degree of an eating disorder, is that:

- They are intensely afraid to be seen as inferior.

- And if they aren't afraid, they are ashamed because they believe they are already inferior.

- Her identity and sense of worth has been unforgivingly defined by body image, whether it's founded on the pride of being thinner, the shame of being fatter, or the illusion that being and eating healthy is what improves your value.

- This entire premise wouldn't exist without giving authority to the graceless belief of thin(ner) supremacy—that the life of thinner bodies is more important and worthy to be lived, than the life of fatter bodies—and that forcing the body to be "healthier" is the superior way to live.

- In this case, people have given the power to define their worth to a narcissistic belief system.

People are taught that in order to be loved and accepted, who they are must become what others approve of, which puts them in a dangerous position to be attracted to people who narcissistically thrive when given authority and power over others.

Request for my help from a woman in her 20's:
Hello Robin, For the past year or so, your online discussions with clients have helped me re-think my attitudes about food, body image, and exercise on my own. Being in your 20s and healthy should not include food and body-image issues. But right now, it does. With how disorganized I have been in the past, I am worried that it is going to spin out of control, and I'm reaching out to you because I'd like some help in reorganizing.

With the way things in life have been going post-college, in and out of jobs, trying to figure things out, the structure of a regular exercise routine and avoiding certain foods has been extremely important for me in order to feel in control, and to stabilize my moods.

While the past two months have been very good—I have been exercising regularly, in varied ways, in addition to eating what I think comes intuitively, and it feels good to be getting stronger and to be feeling better. My problem now is that I am worried because my appetite is increasing, and I am very upset to think of gaining fat. At a normal weight, and slightly above optimal fat percentage, I know it should not matter. But I live in fear that my weight is all going to escalate, especially when I overeat emotionally.

This is so stupid, but I don't want the people at the exercise group I attend to know that I clearly can't keep it together. I am there every day, and so if I don't progress, they will know that it is clearly due to poor nutrition, and right now it really is. Maybe a goal could be to reach out to other members and to talk to them about it, but at this time I really wouldn't be able to do that. Wellbeing wise, I thought I had made progress from earlier in the year, and now I am not sure where it is going, or if I will slowly progress to being in a worse state than where I started.

Chapter 5

Grandiose Narcissism, Co-Narcissism, and Eating Disorders

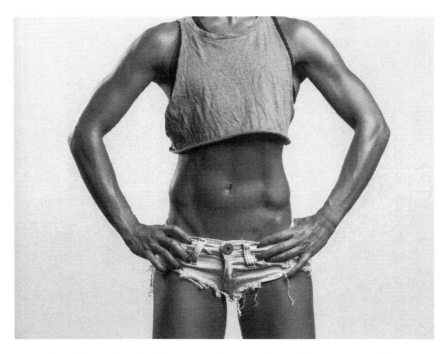

"Don't be afraid of losing people. Be afraid of losing yourself by trying to please everyone around you."

– Author Unknown

Email seeking my help from *a 26-year-old woman raised in a narcissistic family*:

...*When my parents got married, my father demanded my mother quit her job and her college education to stay home and raise the kids, while he brought in the money. She wilfully agreed as she was passive, weak, and submissive back then. We were told her role was to live in the kitchen and be a housewife. I learned to look down on her, and we made fun of and degraded her just like my father did. My mom doesn't realize how unavailable she was when I was growing up, and I still resent her.*

My dad didn't finish high school or go to college because he decided to labor like his father. He's so fake in social settings, trying to make out how proud he is of all his children, but we all feel we will never be good enough for him. He's extremely competitive, controlling and always seeking social approval by trying to morph his kids into something he could never become. Our entire life has centred around keeping my dad from getting angry at us or feeling like we have failed him.

My dad is a misogynist who is racist who puts down and degrades women by what they wear, how they behave, and the attractiveness of their body, etc. One time I overheard him tell my mom he was proud of me because I had such a "tight" bikini body. My mother never stood up for herself or any of us kids when my dad put us down, and she always defended him saying that at least he wasn't physically abusive. I know she was very stressed about making ends meet but his verbal abuse was always excused. Every time I stood up to my dad, he put me down too, saying I'm not a lady or feminine enough. I've learned to relate to all men the same way.

I've braced myself for every guy to react to me the way my dad criticized me with his harsh remarks about every aspect of me (my weight/appearance/education/behaviour as a female). I want to be strong and have boundaries with men, but I'm afraid they won't like me. I minimize myself when I'm with men because that's how I think I have to be. I'm afraid if I'm not submissive, I'll be seen as a pathetic and worthless. If a guy pays attention to me, I'll do anything to keep his attention. I've even studied porn so that I'd be better at sex and what a man wants in order to keep him. Time and time again, I've put myself in dangerous and abusive situations because of my need to be accepted by men.

And I don't feel safe with women either. I get extremely paranoid when I see groups of girls, thinking they are always talking about me and laughing about me. I've never had any true female friends and see them as a threat or as competition for a male. Even when I was in rehab, I was competitive with the other girls. And if there were boys there, I'd do anything to get sexual attention from them. I know I can't move forward from my eating disorder until I address all of this.

I want to get well and be happy like everybody else. I want to move forward with my life—but I still feel like an 11-year-old girl trapped in a 26-year-old's body. I've failed college dozens of times and still don't have a career. I always quit because I'm either going back into the psychiatric unit for my eating disorder or skipping classes doing compulsive exercising at the university gym, or I get distracted by obsessing over a guy whose shown interest in me.

I want to let go of my constant need for approval from men, but I believe for myself that I need to maintain my thinness. To me, being overweight is "butch-looking," and I want to maintain a sense of femininity. I think that for me to feel more like myself, I should be thinner and more petite. I'm afraid if I gain any more weight that there will be no point to doing my hair, my nails, or striving for who I want to be.

If I can't feel good about myself, what's the point in life? I don't even know who I am because my entire identity has been about sex, men, and this eating disorder.

Grandiose and Vulnerable Narcissism

The entire culture of body-image supremacy is dictated by the belief that by attaining the right body you will be special enough to be lovable and worthy of inclusion. Whether it's fit supremacy, health supremacy, athletic supremacy, beauty supremacy, or any other "supremacy" being promoted as a means to being seen as "special" and worthy of acceptance, if your worth is defined by a "superior" belief system, your survival will always be vulnerable and "inferior"—unless they approve of you.

When inclusion isn't based on intrinsic or inherent truth, you are vulnerable to any opinion that decides what your worth should be. Your survival becomes easily influenced and controlled by any grandiose system or person who plays the role of authority.

When it comes to narcissistic belief systems and how people interact with others, there are generally two narcissistic ways a person copes with radical fear of being inferior. She functions 1) as being the controller, the *grandiose* narcissist, or 2) supporting and seeking validation from the controller, the *vulnerable* narcissist.[9]

A person surviving with *grandiose narcissistic* mechanisms maintains a sense of safety by adapting his or her self-concept

to being inherently superior. They have an attitude of, "No matter what the cost, I am, and will always be better than you."

A person surviving with *grandiose narcissistic* mechanisms…

- Typically suffers from fantasies of unlimited success and power, and seeks excessive admiration and feedback that he is indeed, superior.

- Adjusts his mind to find fault in others, doing so in order to maintain his self-concept of supremacy, with the underlying intent to maintain his status of always being in the spotlight of authority.

- Responds aggressively by blaming and often abusing, or intending harm, to those exposing him as "normal" or inferior.

- Insists that people he's associated with meet and support his fantasy-based standards of self-importance.

In a culture dominated by belief systems that play the role of the grandiose narcissist, it would be expected that followers would have predictable signs and symptoms of vulnerability, like children raised by a narcissist. This is where *vulnerable-narcissistic* tendencies arise in people adapting to grandiose narcissist's authoritarian-like demands.

People with *vulnerable-narcissistic* tendencies adapt their identity and way of being to meet standards of supremacy in order to avoid criticism and degradation, to gain acceptance and inclusion, and to "fit in" with people that are apparent authority.[10]

This is different than someone with grandiose narcissism who seeks to dominate and control his sense of self-importance and specialness.

- *Vulnerable narcissists* are subservient, and without question they dogmatically internalize concepts of unforgiving idealism and perfectionism, believing that these high-reaching benchmarks are for their own good and will earn worth, acceptance, and approval.

- Another term used to describe this subservient role is *co-narcissist*. The role of the co-narcissist is to support, confirm, praise, and validate the grandiose narcissist who is dominating and taking ownership of her life.[10]

She's been manipulated and defined in a role with the sole purpose of perfectly mirroring, stroking, and supplying the narcissist's demands and grandiose egotistical needs. A person in the co-narcissistic role or with vulnerable narcissistic traits typically bases her identity and worth on the beliefs, opinions, and standards determined by the authoritarian grandiose narcis-

sists. As a result, she might adapt herself to inhumane standards and expectations that seem narcissistic, but only because those are the principles that she's supposed to obey in order to supply the narcissist his needs or to avoid his vulnerabilities.

Because a person in this position internalizes these demands, she represses and loses touch with her true self, and becomes underdeveloped and unaware of who she is. In doing so, she typically lacks healthy means to express herself, and is deficient in her ability to be self-directed.[10]

As a consequence, people in this vulnerable position gravitate toward rigid controls and rules, and feel lost or "out of control" when left to their own devices.

Any authoritarian system that functions similarly to a grandiose narcissist, like religious cults with dogmatic ideals, will seem safe and attractive to a person who has been a victim of narcissistic abuse.

Alternatively, a person who might not have been conditioned or abused by a narcissistic person, might have been raised to conform to a narcissistic totalitarian system. In this case, when she leaves the system, it would make sense that she'd gravitate to a new but different totalitarian system.

MY EXPERIENCE: *As I failed the rigid and unforgiving rules of the religion I was raised in, I compensated by gravitating to a similar narcissistic system of supremacy through body image. I reinforced thin(ner) supremacy the same way I previously reinforced the religion. My family wasn't hyper-focused on thinness and dieting, so when I turned to controlling my life with being ultra-thin and fit, it didn't necessarily come from my family itself.*

However, looking back, I can see that the totalitarian approach to religion conditioned me to seek a similar totalitarian system when I sought my own sense of survival. At the time, I could easily have been attractive to and manipulated by any grandiose narcissist, but because I was so traumatized by my "immoral" interactions with men, I gravitated to another controlling system rather than a controlling person. I clutched onto body image as if it was my new "special" religion, and my new means to feel lovable.

It's as if the culture of thin(ner) supremacy and the controlling nature of diet industry was a perfect replacement for the iso-

lating fear-based system (religion) by which I was previously conditioned.

Instead of being a co-narcissist with a narcissistic religion, I became a compliant follower seeking approval from a grandiosely narcissistic body image and the diet and fitness industry.

"Bad-You" or "Poor-Me" Victim Defense Mechanisms

In my discussions with people suffering from eating disorders over the years, I have encountered only a handful of people I assume were *grandiose narcissists* who believed they were literally superior people.

People functioning with *grandiose narcissism* typically don't experience as much shame about their body, which decreases their risks of an eating disorder.[11, 12] Although, in terms of maintaining their supremacy, there is a correlation between grandiose narcissism to specific eating disorders such as anorexia, and/or bulimia, and recent studies have shown a strong correlation between orthorexia nervosa and narcissism.[13, 14, 15]

The handful of people I've worked with who positioned themselves in such a grandiose way, were extremely difficult to help. When having to face the vulnerable truth of recovery, they often blamed me for why they feel bad about themselves.

Studies suggest the "bad-you" defense mechanism, where the narcissist views her therapist as being faulty, is common with eating disorders. Especially when identifying truths that expose the individual's vulnerabilities.[14]

Studies suggest that as cognitive dissonance arises, in order to maintain the false front of her superior self-concept, she makes the therapist be wrong, and assumes he or she needs to change and their process needs to be corrected.[14] The attitude is that the person helping just doesn't know how toxic food is, or how valuable and important her perfect body should be, or how horrible her parents were, which is why she deserves to binge eat. They believe simply: *The therapist or coach just doesn't "get it."*

Unsurprisingly, when I pose the idea of gaining weight or being unhealthy to people in this grandiose state of mind, they typically respond angrily toward me—as if asking the question is offensive, stupid, and hurtful.

- One woman even suggested that I was promoting depression and low self-esteem by asking the question.

- After identifying the perpetual "victim state of mind" with another woman, she accused me of being degrading and abusive for even suggesting she look at her martyr response as problematic.

- When I asked one particular client how life would change if recovery required that she permanently accept being unhealthy and/or overweight, her response was that she'd rather suffer horribly in isolation, and then die. When answering the question, she refused to allow herself to think beyond the catastrophe or let go of her protective ego.

Their experience is that I'm poking the sleeping predator in their mind, and provoking the negative feelings their eating disorder is trying to hide. People in this state of mind can't see that their underlying narcissistic supremacy beliefs and inner feelings of weakness and inadequacy are what threatens their survival, and what's bringing up those feelings of victimhood.

Request for my help from a woman in her 30's:

I have written some background information about my situation for you as I am unsure as to whether you are able to help me. I tend to need constant reassurance and need someone to almost argue with me. Many therapists have seen this as me refusing to budge my attitude, but I think it is more that my eating disorder is putting up a fight, but surely this is a good thing that I keep trying to find help. I want someone to argue against these things, and I need someone to change my mind about the eating disorder. I want to end this problem as it is dominating and running my life. I seem unable to fight it on my own for any significant amount of time. Most of the people who I have worked with previously give up and say they can't help me. Please let me know if you are open to working with me.

Each and every person I talk to who suffers with an eating disorder eventually experiences anger and rage when asked to surrender the coping mechanisms that give her the illusion of safety. Although, most clients don't project that anger at me like the grandiose type. It's more foreseeable that people respond with a "poor-me" victim position.

Research on the topic has shown that people with eating disorders commonly display signs of "poor-me" narcissistic defense mechanisms, or play the "martyr" in order to deflect responsibility. They don't want to feel the shame and inferiority that arises without their eating disorder to protect them.[15]

When asked how life would change if she had to remain overweight or obese, or had to gain more weight, most people (unlike grandiose narcissists) are more willing to face the truth of the answer, even when it might bring about feelings of loss, shame, or embarrassment. Instead of responding offensively or in anger, they allow their feelings about it to come forward, and by and large, *their response is based in shame, and the fear of being seen as worthless by others.* They are more concerned about being criticized and looked down upon, and their vulnerability to being rejected, than they are the horrendous suffering they live while clutching onto their eating disorder.

Whether it's fear and shame of being too weak to handle life without eating, or being inferior and worthless without having a thinner body—self-pity for having to face the truth triggers the cycle that perpetuates the desire for the eating disorder from which they're trying to recover.

> **Observing this response has brought me to believe that by and large, most people suffering with eating disorders are actually showing symptoms of vulnerable narcissism, or co-narcissism.**

Link Between Vulnerable Narcissism and Eating Disorders

Study after study shows a strong link between vulnerable narcissism and eating disorders.[9, 11, 12, 13, 14, 15, 16, 17, 18] By far, the bulk of clients I work with don't see others as inferior and promote themselves as superior, but rather internally they feel inferior within themselves and are striving to earn approval, like a co-narcissist held captive by the grandiose narcissist.

In this position, you don't naturally think of yourself as superior or better than others, though you are seeking inclusion and safety by being accepted as superior.

> **NOTE:** A common comment from my clients when discussing narcissism and thin(ner) supremacy is: "I truly don't feel better than people who are overweight. They deserve love, care, and kindness. I have friends and family who are larger than me, and

I would never define them by their weight. However, if I am overweight, I feel terrible about myself. And I feel terrible when I'm around people who are thinner than me. I want to shrink and hide."

You might have enough compassion for others to believe they deserve the freedom to be themselves, and to be loved. But when it comes to yourself, there is no compassion, and in order to deserve the same love and acceptance, you are held to much higher unforgiving standards. To me this is a sign a person's self-concept has been assimilated to perform for approval by some form of *controlling grandiose narcissism.*

People surviving with *vulnerable narcissism:*

- Rely on validation and feedback from others to define their lovability.

- Become hypersensitive to the opinions of others.

- Often base their safety from rejection by reinforcing concepts of superiority within themselves.

- Become clutching or clingy to the approval when given compliments.

- Respond in shame and humiliation when they are criticized.

- Internalize their inadequacy as personal indications of inferiority and weakness.

Their reaction is very different than the grandiose narcissist, as they don't react in rage or fighting—but instead they withdraw, hide, and avoid real (or imagined) ridicule.

Request for my help from a woman in her 30's:
I have huge shame attached to the fact that I've recently gained 30 pounds. I've avoided my in-laws because they haven't seen me since I was skinny, which is quite a feat. My father-in-law is very looks-and-image focused, and I just can't bear to see his face when he sees me. I used his reaction as a motivator for losing weight in the first place. Now I just can't seem to lose weight, because I'm burnt out, and nothing I seem to do can get my head in the right place. Help!

Narcissism and Body Image

With respect to body image, people with vulnerable-narcissistic tendencies often seek to improve their self-worth through the enhancement of their physical appearance.[9, 18] In a culture that promotes worth based on narcissistic thin(ner) supremacy, it would make sense that a believer seeking approval would have survival-oriented determination to achieve a thinner body in order to feel worthy of inclusion and also safe from rejection. And if she doesn't meet the body-image ideals, she would experience a higher rate of fear and shame, and in turn, hide or isolate herself from exposure until her body is fixed.

Her survival-oriented desires to be loved and accepted through reaching narcissistic ideals such as thin(ner) supremacy, magnifies the urge to measure and monitor her size and weight in comparison to the thinner-than-normal standard. And in coordination, her fear of disapproval and rejection projects onto food as if eating endangers her acceptability and makes her worthy of disapproval and rejection. As a consequence, *she eats in fear and wants food in shame.*

> **In essence, primal survival mechanisms, like magnified tunnel vision, heightened senses, and other cognitive distortions, make her perceptions of food and her body more urgent and sensitive.**

This coincides with research suggesting that people with vulnerable-narcissistic traits tend to objectify their bodies, as if their looks are meant for other people's pleasure.[11] In cultures that accept narcissistic standards of thinness for women as attractive, you could expect much higher levels of body shame with respect to body shape, weight, and size. Studies suggest when a person is invalidated, especially by their parents, he or she's likely to seek an alternative way to receive validation through dogmatic body images like thin(ner) supremacy. This *vulnerable narcissistic search for validation through body image is a risk factor for eating disorders.*[11, 12] This means that a person might lean on thin(ner)-supremacy belief systems to find her validation, when she doesn't receive validation from important people, like her parents. I assume important social groups can be invalidating too.

> **MY EXPERIENCE:** *For me, it wasn't that my parents didn't provide security and validation, but the religious guidelines they raised me by required a high standard of living in order to earn that validation. When I failed to adhere to the grandiose standards of that "superior" religion, I internalized that failure as a sign I was unworthy. I assumed my parents would invalidate me too. In shame, I turned to body images of fitness, thinness, and health to supplement the validation I believed I had lost. Instead of dedicating my identity to a totalitarian-style religion, I turned to body images and applied myself to them with the same unforgiving authoritarian-style approach. The truth is my parents love me dearly, and had*

they known the darkness I was in, they would have given me grace from adhering to the religion they raised me to identify myself by.

Survival Mode, Body Image, and Food

Not fitting in, and the shame attached to negative body image, is a central fear to every single person I've worked with who suffers with an eating disorder. Whether she/he's orthorexic, anorexic, bulimic, or suffering with binge eating disorder, fear and shame attached to losing a superior body image is foundational to his/her toxic relationship with food.

This has led me to believe that:

- A person suffering with an eating disorder is actually suffering from severe threat to primitive survival mechanisms, and the disorder is triggered by internal feelings of inadequacy that promotes more intense fears of abandonment, rejection, and permanent disproval and shame.

- These fears are directly related to our innate need to be included, loved, and valued by our family and friends, as a way to validate a position of security in our community.

- Without that security, the life the body gives, and the freedom to live it, gets hijacked by the intense survival-oriented work necessary to hide and repress those fears of inferiority and rejection.

The threat of abandonment and rejection from narcissistic cultures of body-image supremacy alerts a person's survival mechanisms when a believer isn't able to eat "healthy," lose weight, or remain thin. This manifests as an urge to micro-manage perceived "dangers" in food and with her food intake.

These fears about the "dangers" of eating promote that she chronically restrict food, resort to excessive dieting, and have a preoccupation with her weight, size, and shape of her body.[14, 17] Ultimately, mechanisms wired to protect one's access to food get triggered, and she'll have rising desires, needs, and motivations to eat that go beyond "normal" eating patterns.

Ask yourself:

✓ Who determines what defines being thin enough, healthy enough, and what defines the image of the body we are to strive for?

✓ Who are we trying to gain approval from?

Request to work with me from a woman in her late 30's:
I am desperate for help. I am 37 and have been on a diet or in binge mode literally since the second grade. I have been in so many programs I can't even count. I have been diagnosed with OCD, Bulimia and Binge Eating Disorder. I have weighed from 130 pounds to 320 pounds and everywhere in between. Right now, I am currently gaining and am 225 pounds, and I am 5'7.

I don't know what to do, I can't afford $40,000 to go into an inpatient treatment center. Also, I am getting a lot of reactions such as...since I am not too thin, I am not really sick. WHAT THE HELL. I would really like the chance to work with you if possible. I am at the end of my rope and I think it was not an accident that I found your videos online.

IMPORTANT: Clearly there's conflict between the pressure to be thinner and the natural need to want security with food.

Any narcissistic culture promoting unnatural physical standards as the means to be accepted would eventually have resultant psychological and physical "illness" that is culture-wide with believers—particularly, physical standards that directly threaten other biological needs to survive, like how the worship of thinness conflicts with followers' ability to eat.

When survival fears of exclusion, rejection, and abandonment require that a person restrict and deprive food, she activates an even-more powerful survival mechanism that is set to need food in order to stay alive.

When these two evolved life needs intertwine to work with each other or to compete with each other—*that is what I believe promotes eating disorders*. And because the issue is multifaceted, I question if the issue is more of a "syndrome" than a "disorder."

However, this only makes sense in societies where food is largely abundant, easily accessed, and perpetually available. Without excess food, ultra-lean bodies wouldn't be seen as superior, and restricting oneself into starvation wouldn't be distorted into a moral virtue.

Chapter 6

Survival Mode for the Privileged

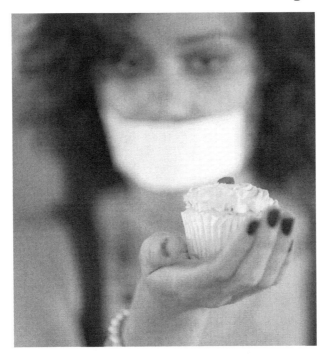

"When ideologically isolated, we experience our problems, thoughts, and feelings as unique to us as individuals. As a result, we are prevented from recognizing the social/political basis of our situations and problems."

– Dee L.R. Graham, *Loving to Survive: Sexual Terror, Men's Violence, and Women's Lives*

Today, we have more food than we could ever need, but for some reason many people have been convinced:

- The only way we can relax around food and enjoy that abundance is if we do or achieve something to earn it.

- If you don't achieve or accomplish anything and still eat, you're looked at as entitled and selfish. To enjoy the pleasure of food, you must earn it first.

- People who are thought to have too much fat are looked at as if they don't deserve to be fed, no matter what. They are expected to restrict food and if they don't, they are shamed and criticized.

- Thinner people are perceived as having superior strength and discipline for not eating as much. They are praised and looked up to as elite examples of self-control and beauty.

- If thinner people do eat and stay thin, they are seen as having superior bodies.

I assume this is how an insecure community of people in scarcity would ration a hoard of food among their members. But we are doing it with large masses of food that doesn't need to be rationed. The question is, who and what decides who deserves to eat and who doesn't? What earns a person the status of being seen as more valuable and worthy of life than another?

For most people in rich cultures, access to food doesn't depend on someone else determining if we deserve to eat or not, but in a psychological state of scarcity, people are still wired to think this way.

When looking at the entire premise of the narcissistic culture of thin(ner) supremacy, what determines a person's right to eat is if she is thin enough. When she's thin enough, what determines her status among thinner people is if she has the will power and control to continue eating less. I assume that this problem would only exist in cultures of relative advantage, the ones with more abundance and wealth than our evolutionary psychology has adapted to.

Request for my help from a 37-year-old woman:
I have been dieting all my life. It started when I was a child. Recently, I was on a protein diet for the last two years and then regained all the weight I lost. I had a lap-band procedure but had it removed because of slippage. The doctor kicked me out when I asked for a sleeve surgery as I am not obese. I am suicidal, and I am praying for a solution. I just can't do this anymore.

The Privilege of Thin and Health Supremacy

Eating-disordered feelings and behaviors linked to thinness only make sense if you radically believe body fat is bad, food is bad, and that you and your body are bad and are in danger unless you control both. From my personal experience, this is a complex, complicated, and multifaceted problem that to outsiders who don't think this way, seems crazy. *It is crazy.* However, from the inside, it makes perfect sense and to not think or be that way under the circumstance would seem foolish.

To not overeat or binge, when it seems food is going to be permanently taken from you, would be weird. To not puke or exercise after overeating, when you believe eating too much is dangerously toxic, would be bizarre.

It would be unwise not to precisely measure and control the food you eat when it feels like uncontrolled eating will destroy your health, your worth, your reputation, and your life.

> **Within the walls of this dark survival-oriented space, what seems "disordered" to outsiders, is perfectly safe and justifiable based on the distress people feel on the inside.**

It only seems bizarre when it's obvious a person is more panicked than the evidence suggests, and it takes over his or her life. This is like when a person describes feelings of panic of being starved as they binge prior to thinking they're going to diet. Or it's how a person thinks she's gained too much body fat when she's demonstrably ultra-lean. I assume this is largely due to believing media, propaganda, and fear-based belief systems that support, encourage, and give credibility to this way of thinking. More often than not, panic is encouraged as being healthy by people making money and gaining power by proselytizing this "space of survival" as narcissistically superior—as if people who don't panic are stupid or dumb and will regret it later.

Eventually, more vigilant followers are willing to admit something is wrong as they suffer miserably in their "safe" isolation and darkness. If they're willing to reach out for help, more often than not, sufferers are told they have a genetic disease or an addiction that they'll likely struggle with for the rest of their life. When emotional support and guidance comes from people who also believe that fear-based system within themselves, it makes sense they'd assume the perfectionism, misery, and struggle must come from personal problems that need to be worked out or a genetic disease they'll have to learn to live with.

MY EXPERIENCE: *When I finally reached out for help, that's what I was told, and for me the assumption that I'd suffer with an eating disorder the rest of my life further supported my urges to* *commit suicide. I think back to my dark-and-demented eating disorder space and wonder:*

— *If it was a genetic disease, what type of therapy or medication would have been powerful enough to remove my desire to and excitement about organizing and controlling my food intake?*

— *What would be strong enough to stop the euphoria of bingeing before and after I failed and restarted another perfectionistic restrictive diet?*

— *What would have reduced how much I cared about the food I ate, taken away the excitement about my goal to weigh under 150 pounds, and to fit a size 6 in jeans?*

— *What medication would reduce my determined sense of accomplishment, as well as the safety I felt after burning 1000 calories with exercise every day?*

— *What type of pill or therapy would have made it so that I didn't feel terror and a sense of looming death if I gained body fat?*

The answer is that nothing could have done any of that for me, because my beliefs about myself and my body in relation to my life would have had to change.

I know this: had I been dropped off to survive in a country suffering in poverty, disease, and famine, where access to food is a luxury, and body fat is a lifesaving need, I would have completely snapped out of that belief system so fast that I would have had an instantaneous release from the disorder.

That experience would have dissolved the fantasy I was chasing,

123

and made the destructive behavior I was using to survive an obvious form of torture and abuse. In other words, exposure to true life-and-death situations would undistort the made-up illusions of "danger" that's created in an existence isolated in privilege and abundance.

When generations are fortunate enough to have access to large amounts of food in overflowing abundance, and are perpetually advantaged to where they've never experienced true scarcity that results in widespread starvation, there's a large distance that's created—separating true and real danger with food from perceived made-up danger. Generations lose touch with reality as they gain touch with conceptualized made-up realities.

This distance increases as people's internal sense of ability to handle threat decreases because he or she is removed from factual exposure and experience that would allow an inner sense of capacity to develop. At the same time, as people are shielded from their own vulnerability, a sense of capacity can develop within that sheltered state of abundance, which results in a sense of danger if that abundance is threatened. In the end, survival mechanisms wired to responds to actual threat gets triggered in environments that are above and beyond safe and sheltered, and are excessively insulated from factual danger.

People begin to create beliefs, fears, and problems that wouldn't exist without their relative wealth and abundance. For example, the way people are encouraged to look at food under a microscope to make sure it's "healthy," would be seen as ridiculous if that same exact food was keeping you and your family alive during wide-spread famine.

Food labeled as "bad" and toxic by people who hold themselves to an idealistic diet image, would eat that same "toxic" food without thought if their food supply became scarce.

Idealistic diet beliefs lose effect when food is scarce. When you look at food morality and restrictive eating as a "lifestyle," you are witnessing privilege in action. The same goes for fitness and exercise methods that most followers don't understand require a certain level of privilege too. And the worship of thinness as a symbol of superiority, health, and sexual attractiveness is a narcissistic viewpoint that requires absolute ignorance from true survival reality where food, medical care, and immunizations are scarce.

The entire premise of health(ier) and thin(ner) supremacy are beliefs that stem from generations being sheltered with easy access to large amounts of food in abundance, and from never having experienced the radical damages of pandemics, diseases, and viruses that exist without the advantage of vaccines, running clean water, soap, and basic cleanliness.

The choice to remove animal products from your eating "lifestyle," or only eating high fat/low carb, or juicing large amounts of fruits and vegetables, committing to a 30-day cleanse, or timing and proportioning food consumption to burn more calories, etc.—all require that believers live in an abundance of food. Of course, there are negative consequences that come from excessive eating over long periods of time or from being overly sedentary. Nonetheless, the option of being able to pick and choose what supplements we take, the type of fitness activities we want to do, or a lifestyle of how we restrict food *is a privilege* that for many people has become distorted into being a sign of moral supremacy. That arrogance is then capitalized on by businesses selling their "lifestyle" as if it's necessary in order to be respected, loved, and safe in a concept of "health" they've defined for you.

Because we've been fortunate to not experience widespread famine and death by starvation, body fat has been distorted and stigmatized as disgusting and dangerous, and restricting food is seen as a sanctimonious symbol of superior self-control. Because of this, it's very difficult for people to see that eating disorders like the one I suffered in, might be survival mechanisms functioning perfectly inside cultures that are advantaged with food and sheltered from famine.

Ask Yourself: Would the worship of thinness and shaming of fat gain exist in cultures suffering in widespread poverty,

- Where ultra-leanness is commonplace, which is a negative quality when it comes to surviving illness?

- Where not eating enough or "dieting" isn't a choice or sign of superiority or as a healthy "lifestyle?"

- Where there isn't food available that you can eat excessively in order to escape negative or stressful life circumstances?

When isolated from real danger, people can easily create alternative ideas of danger that can only exist in wealth, abundance, and naive ignorance. To undistort those types of irrational fears so they are more truthfully aligned with our evolutionary wiring, people would need to expose themselves to the truth of life, removed from the option of those advantages.

Comparison allows a person to recognize the distortions that make things seem dangerous when they're factually not. With that said, when comparing cultures that live more closely to survival reality, to cultures that live in isolation from that reality, it would make sense that without true life-and-death context, the privileged people would show signs of survival attachment to their luxuries and wealth.

> **MY EXPERIENCE:** *For me, being made aware of the truth didn't require that I get dropped off to survive in a country suffering in drought and famine, but that I recognize my life would be better free from the confinement of that privilege. It was safer for me to*

surrender the safety of my survival than to die clutching to my "perfect body." Freedom came to me when I compared the misery and suffering of the eating disorder I was living in, to the death I was about to experience by suicide. **When death was a relief, the terror that my eating disorder served lost its power.**

Is it Really a Disorder about Eating?

When the body images that are dogmatically accepted require followers to radically manipulate and restrict food, it would seem as if people suffering from an unusual obsession and preoccupation with dieting and food might have an "eating disorder."

> **What goes unnoticed, however, is the survival attachment to narcissistic concepts of thin(ner) supremacy—especially when those who are studying eating issues believe in that particular body image too.**

As multiple generations have been raised in enough safety and privilege to praise body images that aspire to attain superior thinness, fitness, and concepts of exceptional "health," it's understandable why early researchers studying eating disorders wouldn't notice that the narcissistic worship of thinner people, and the stigma and derogative shaming of fatter people, might be attributing significantly to people's issues with food. This is particularly true when therapists in that same privilege have probably also internalized those same body images as more superior within themselves. Today, the level of study regarding body image and the connection to eating issues certainly helps us with that clarity, thanks to people looking outside the paradigm *that eating disorders are a food-derived problem.*

When looking at eating disorders, feasting and famine behaviors don't seem disordered at all when seeing the threat to both a person's access to food and the drive to diet, as a means to mitigate threats of inadequacy and abandonment. Even the drive to attain a body image isn't disordered when you look at it as an evolutionary protective mechanism to blend in or fit in with your society.

What's disordered is the goal to meet images and ideas that are completely inhumane and unrealistic. It's the grandiosely narcissistic nature of the images people are challenged to dogmatically follow that are so harmful and "mentally ill."

Even so, what propels someone to overreach with such perfectionistic extremes still makes sense based on primitive mechanisms that are radically triggered to fight to stay alive—markedly, when access to available survival needs is controlled by an authority who only approves those who dogmatically perform beyond their natural human capacity.

Request for my help from a woman in her 20s:
Hi Robin. I am an actress with bulimia. I have been listening to your videos and was trying to figure out how to stop this whole madness with dieting, bingeing, purging etc. But because my work is dependent on how I look, I am extremely obsessive about my body image. I also come from abusive family. My sister always glorified how skinny she was, and she'd put me down because of my weight. My father dated skinny women and told me that I would never succeed if I didn't lose weight. I have been trying to lose weight and abuse myself with bingeing and purging starting at age 12. And only after watching your videos have I realized that instead of making my life happen, I am stuck in my pattern of bulimia and obsessing about my weight. If I gain weight I don't come out of my house. Anyways, I wanted to talk to you about what to do when your body, and the way you look, is your career.

Surviving with an Eating Disorder

As extreme fixation on eating and food controls are the obvious behavioral outcomes for people who fear negative perceptions of their bodyfat, I believe these survival behaviors might be mislabeled as "disordered" when in reality they indicate healthy survival mechanisms that are functioning as they should. The problem is that without understanding what emotions and needs the obsessive-compulsive survival motivations supply, they seem bizarre and unnecessary when our environment is full of bounty, safety, and abundance in all aspects of survival. When looking at it from the context of survival and supposed danger, clearly the behavior comes from perceptions of threat that don't necessarily exist in reality.

I believe the behavioral symptoms of eating disorders might be compulsions stemming from survival mechanisms that have been triggered outside of normal context.

Given the appropriate evolutionary survival context, it makes sense why:

- Someone would isolate herself from "dangerous" food in order to force her body to be superior in its "health" or thinness.

- A bulimic would puke her food up or turn to extreme exercise when she believes weight gain will threaten her approval from others.

- Someone would binge when the shame she has about her size, health, and weight puts her in a position to overeat in preparation for being shunned into the "wilderness," and when under radical pressure to diet to make things right.

All of these actions are clearly modes of self-defense, and the only reason these behaviors seem "disordered" is because we don't live in the wilderness or in widespread famine, and we aren't eating poisonous food where these mechanisms would align with true life-and-death threats.

These survival mechanisms are being triggered, even though we live in privilege and abundance compared to environments where these mechanisms evolved.

Instead of assuming that people who binge lack willpower, education, desire, work ethic, and are addicted to food, recognize that they are struggling and lack the capacity to reverse tens of thousands of years of evolved survival mechanisms that are triggered by perceptions of deprivation and famine. Better understanding comes when looking at these impulses and obsessions from the view of survival mode and Maslow's Hierarchy of Needs.

The same applies when trying to understand why a person would willfully die of starvation when food is readily available. It helps to recognize that her food restriction positively supports a sense of safety and control in a narcissistic culture that not only shames, ridicules, stigmatizes, and hates body fat, but also degrades "bad" and unhealthy eating. To her, restricting food keeps her safe from intense death threats coming from the narcissistic body-image "cult" mentality. *This dangerously flips the focus away from thinness to survive, to starving to survive, as if her willingness to refuse food is what keeps her safe from the terror of death.*

For a binge eater, not eating would feel that same way, despite his or her body gaining more and more body fat to the point of physical disability. This is similar to how a person who's self-righteous and sanctimonious about eating "healthy" or "clean" food, might fear "unhealthy" or "dirty" food. If she omits a large range of "bad" food from being eaten, she limits her ability to eat socially and also predisposes herself to nutritional deficiencies and susceptibility to illness for that reason.

Her loyalty and reliance on dieting or bingeing, although posing incredible danger to her life, is similar to the loyalty a battered wife has with her abuser, or a prisoner might have with her captor. This might be due to a survival defense mechanism commonly described as *Stockholm Syndrome*.

This is a phenomenon that occurs under certain circumstances where a prisoner forms affection for her captor, and willfully obeys and defends his abusive demands. She eventually identifies safety with her captor because to her, accommodating him equates to less harm and increased hope for life. Even when the demands are destructive and harmful, loyalty and affection for her dangerous captor feels like the safest way to stay alive.

In the case of eating disorders, unforgiving narcissistic body images are the authoritarian captor that's been given totalitarian control over his or her access to food and survival. The eating disorder is what she must do as a consequence to stay alive.

———————————————————

Message from a woman in her 30's:
I'm a career dieter and feel like I have a food addiction. I've sought out every type of therapy and have NEVER EVER heard the approach you take to help people. You are the first person I've heard articulated perfectly the way I've felt. It's an amazing feeling to hear out loud what you feel constantly 24/7—but have been in the dark about. The way you describe the pressure and torment to fix my body linked to the continuous thoughts of unworthiness is so true. It is an amazing feeling to hear someone voice the way you feel, when you don't have to words to speak for yourself. And when I say amazing, I mean it.

From what you've described about your recovery, it seems to me that we come from similar backgrounds with strict religious up-

bringing. I still believe and hold the core fundamentals true to my heart, but I understand the judgment you speak about. When I'm around my family, especially my mom, her judgment is excruciating. She makes me so nervous and I have lots of anxiety when I'm around her. After watching your YouTube videos, I can see now that my issues with food and my body are directly tied to my desire to feel good about my religious failings. I could go on and on...so let me end here. God certainly lead me to your YouTube channel. Thank you so much! You are my angel!!

SECTION 3

Killing Yourself to Survive: Stockholm Syndrome, and Complex PTSD

"For me, my awakening came when I was kidnapped."

– Patty Hearst, Survivor of Stockholm Syndrome

Chapter 7

Trauma Bonding and Stockholm Syndrome

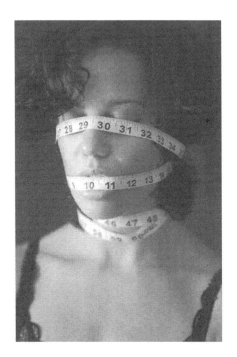

"Kind slaveholders may have made slavery more bearable for their slaves but that did not make the institution of slavery any less heinous."

– Dee L.R. Graham, *Loving to Survive: Sexual Terror, Men's Violence, and Women's Lives*

Body-Diet Supremacy Syndrome

According to *Merriam-Webster Dictionary*, the definition of disorder is: *"An abnormal physical or mental condition."*

The definition of syndrome is: *"A group of signs and symptoms that occur together and characterize a particular abnormality or condition."*

There is a distinct difference between the definitions. They both are an abnormal condition, but with a syndrome the abnormal result occurs when a combination of conditions "run together." Without that combination, the abnormal result goes away or doesn't occur. When looking at eating disorders as a syndrome, there are five possible conditions I can point out that I think combine to form the eating-disorder "syndrome."

1. Large abundance and wealth of food that insulates a society from the risk and awareness of environmental famine and uncontrollable starvation.

2. A personal position of needing external validation from others to secure his or her third hierarchy of need: to feel worthy of love, inclusion, and acceptance.

3. Traumatic interpersonal experience that would lead to shame-based self-soothing, punishment, and other coping mechanisms used to hide from or fight internalized stigma and fears of rejection and abandonment.

4. Identifying primarily, or more heavily by narcissistic body images as a means to secure one's third hierarchy of need to earn love, inclusion, and acceptance.

- A form of measurement is needed to compare her body to the ideal image, i.e., circumference measurements, weight, body fat percentages, clothing size, visual cues like hip bones, ribs, collar bones, or thigh gaps. This might include measurements such as burned calories, resting metabolic rates, resting heart rate, blood pressure, etc. With concepts of "health" that can't necessarily be measured, people use some form of measurable supply, like an organized diet or exercise routine. This is the next condition attributing to the syndrome.

5. Identifying primarily, or more heavily by narcissistic "diet images" as a means to supply measurement and controls for a superior body image. Food restriction necessitates additional support, strictness, isolation, controls and measurements to repress increased urges to eat as one's first hierarchy of need is triggered as insecure.

- This includes one or more means of control, like the promise of continued and more strict dieting after eating is allowed, narcissistic exercise images, diuretic abuse, purging, chewing and spitting out food, appetite suppressants, nutritional supplementation abuse, etc.

I assume the more of these conditions a person has, the more intense her syndrome might be. With these combined, you could say a person's eating disorder symptoms would be the result of her "Body- and Diet-Image Supremacy Stockholm Syndrome" or what might be more appropriately called *"Body-Diet Supremacy Syndrome."*

NOTE: I am fully aware there could be more conditions that significantly contribute to an eating disorder *as a syndrome.* However, I am not an expert, and people who are more knowledgeable might be better at identifying the conditions and appropriately naming the syndrome.

As the previous chapters talked about the privilege of abundance and the insecurity to a person's first and third hierarchies of need, in this and the next chapter, I will discuss the aspects of the other conditions listed that I think are contributing factors. To start, I'll describe psychological syndromes that I think eating disorders are similar to.

Stockholm Syndrome and Trauma Bonding

Stockholm Syndrome is a psychological phenomenon where a hostage shows loyalty and affection for her captor, even when she's being harmed and abused. In 1973, the term Stockholm Syndrome was coined by Nils Bejerot, a criminologist and psychiatrist who was asked to analyze the bizarre mental state of the victims taken hostage during a bank robbery in Stockholm, Sweden. The victims were held captive in one of the bank's vaults for six days, and despite their lives being threatened they developed a compassionate bond and alliance with the bank robbers. Their minds were so wrapped around the safety gained by sympathizing and accommodating their captors that they then feared the police that were seeking to save their lives, and they defended and maintained intimate relationships with their captors when they were released.

Stockholm Syndrome has also been termed "Trauma Bonding" because of similar bonding that occurs in abusive relationships that aren't necessarily acute hostage situations. According to scientists, trauma bonding has been observed in victims of kidnappings, prisoners of war, physically and/or emotionally abused children, battered women, cult members, victims of totalitarian political and religious oppression, human trafficking, concentration camp prisoners, slaves, and prostitutes.[20]

The victim is aware of the abuse, but because she identifies that her survival relies on the abuser, she yearns for and seeks comfort from him. Her third hierarchy of need is locked in on and honed to please the source of her trauma, to the point where any slight act of mercy (even if she's still abused, but abused less) is magnified in her mind as him being generous, kind, and loving.

Kindness serves as the cornerstone of Stockholm Syndrome because the condition will not develop unless the captor exhibits kindness in some form toward the hostage. If the captor is purely evil and abusive, the hostage will respond with hatred. But, if the perpetrators show some hints of mercy, the victims will repress the anger they feel in response to the terror, and concentrate on the captors' "good side" to protect themselves. "Do what I say and…

- "I'll let you sleep longer,"

- "You'll have my permission to go outside,"

- "You'll get more food," or

- "I won't hurt you."

These are examples of coercions that treat life-sustaining needs as rewards, not as human rights. These "rewards" seem generous when the person in control is fully capable of and could easily choose to inflict harm.

The more she's isolated with him and the more he controls her food, water, sleep, and shelter, the more it seems as if he's being kind to her when he gives her food, lets her rest, or doesn't hurt her or doesn't punish her as severely. And when she is punished, hurt, and restricted for not complying, she will blame herself *because she wasn't perfect.*

The appearance that she had choices in the matter of doing exactly what he needs, makes it seem as if it's her fault when she's punished.

But her only safe choice is to do everything he demands, *to perfection,* in order to survive—especially if he controls her access to her first two hierarchies of needs (food and safety).

The longer a person is isolated and under inescapable totalitarian control, the more she is codependent and thus positively attaches her survival to appeasing her abuser, and thus the more fearful and negative she feels about leaving him. This is particularly true when the victim holds the fantasy that the more she loves and obeys her abuser, his maltreatment of her will eventually stop, and they will live happily together. Because of this, the victim is more likely to stay or return to her abuser, and will be less willing to leave or escape when given the opportunity.

Scientist Celia Jameson suggests that feelings of affection and bonding with an abuser occur as a survival strategy, providing hope for reduced threat and terror through compliance and agreement with the captor.[21]

When you're threatened with abandonment, abuse, or death unless you do what you're told, but are also rewarded or punished less if you obey, the combination of apparent danger with perceived acts of kindness when you comply, cradles the victim's mind to perceive the abuser's needs are her only source of freedom and power.

Even if there isn't an eminent direct threat of danger and torture, when being disapproved of poses an increased threat to a person's working ability to supply vital life needs, such as food or shelter, *disapproval is essentially an indirect death threat.* This phenomenon has been seen in cases of "Corporate Stockholm Syndrome" where an employer controls people's livelihood as well as their work reputation, which determines the worker's potential to find work elsewhere. Developed similarly to Stockholm Syndrome, employees can adapt over time to identify their survival with and be deeply loyal to a job—despite working in an environment that is harmful and abusive.

Basically, the employer governs the employees' fundamental survival needs indirectly by controlling the worker's paycheck and career reputation. Because of threats and intimidations, the worker can be manipulated into working longer hours, accepting verbal and/or sexual abuse, breaking the law, and having her wellbeing and her family's needs ignored. The illusion the job holds the key to her career and livelihood creates confusion about boundaries when what she's asked to do crosses the line into being toxic and abusive. The only way out would be to quit and accept that her reputation will be tarnished.

If one person could develop symptoms of "Corporate Stockholm Syndrome," it's plausible that if the entire environment of a business similarly functioned abusively, there would be a trend of these symptoms in more employees. The same could apply to large groups of people, like in religious cults or in totalitarian cultures that manipulate and enslave its members to identify by harmful traditions. These traditions are a way for members to gain inclusion in order to access life needs such as food, water, and shelter. In this case it would be a form of "Societal Stockholm Syndrome" or "Cultural Trauma Bonding."

Request from woman in her 40's who is an anchor at a major news network:

Hi Robin, it was recommended that I contact you in regard to helping me with an issue I'm struggling with. To be honest, this is an issue I've had for a long time, but for the past two years it has gotten far worse, and I'm starting to have a problem controlling myself.

Since growing up dancing ballet, I've always been concerned about my weight and body image. I've suffered from mainly anorexia, but over the years it has turned into bulimia.

Being thin and attractive has benefitted me in my life, especially in high school. I always felt my body kept me in the spotlight. Today, I am literally in the spotlight as an anchor at (unnamed) news network—and my binge eating and bulimia has spiraled out of control. It is known that the slenderness of the women is an attribute for the news station, and the clothing made available for us in our dressing room is made to highlight this. The problem is: I feel like I'm addicted to sugar, and I am eating too much.

Lately, I've had a more difficult time controlling myself. I make it a day or two eating as little as possible, but eating candy seems to give me the energy I need when writing or doing research. Once I get home I usually binge, and to control my weight, I either puke or use laxatives. My issue is that because I've started to lose control over my eating, I've gained about 10–15 pounds—and the dresses I've been fitted to wear, are too tight. I'm fearful I'll lose my position if I gain any more weight, and there's already been comments in the dressing room about my size. The crazy thing is that I know a couple other anchors here who also have eating disorders, and it makes me cringe to think they are more successful at dieting and staying thinner than I am.

I've had a chance to watch some of your YouTube videos, and I know what you are saying is true. I can tell you've also dealt with this before. But I'm terrified I will lose my job if I gain any more weight. And the more I think about letting this all go, I feel like I am a worthless failure. I can't stop striving to be thinner, so how do I stop bingeing? The ways that I've managed my weight don't seem to be working anymore and I feel like I'm losing my mind.

I'm angry, depressed, and I hate my body this way. I hate it. I'd rather suffer from anorexia and bulimia than be fat.

Cultural Trauma Bonding and "Body-Diet Supremacy Syndrome"

"The more women need comfort and support, the more likely we are to bond to men when men provide them, even if the comfort and support provided are minimal. In fact, the less support we are given, the more dependent we become and the more grateful we are for any crumbs of kindness."

– Dee L.R. Graham, *Loving to Survive: Sexual Terror, Men's Violence, and Women's Lives*

An example of this is how radical body images throughout history have indirectly controlled and threatened access of an entire gender or class of people's survival needs by stigmatizing them as unworthy of inclusion, acceptance, and love if they don't or can't comply. Like foot binding in China's past, which was passed down generation after generation—for over 1,000 years until banned in 1912.

In China, adequately binding your daughter's feet from infancy to where they measured less than 5 inches long, determined how she was to be valued for marriage. But in doing so, her feet became so deformed that she was too disabled to support herself and became entirely reliant on others to survive. The smaller her feet measured, the more she attracted wealthier families to court her, and this meant that they could afford to pay so she was adequately supported. The more that parents disfigured their daughter, the more likely she was to "survive." Unfortunately, if her feet weren't quite small enough, she was seen as unattractive and less valuable for marriage, despite the fact that she was made to live in permanent pain and disability. As the entire culture dogmatically believed and supported this body image, it makes sense why parents would obsess over ways to effectively bind their daughter's feet in order to compete with other girls whose feet might be smaller. Foot binding and other body images in history are discussed in more depth in *Thin-Supremacy*.

Today, this is no different than multiple generations encouraging girls to restrict food and diet to "bind" her body into being "healthier," smaller, and leaner.

In cultures that dogmatically believe women are subservient to men and that men should be the sole provider of food and shelter, it makes sense that women would bond her survival to standards or rules that increase her chances of attraction and marriage. As sexual drive is an important aspect of human nature, being sexually attractive would seem like a securing quality. If a woman doesn't believe she can independently support herself, or that she doesn't have any other attractive assets, she will seek to control her survival by internalizing body images as if it is the only power she has to support her life.

In this case, she bonds with a body image as her security or "job," and her employer is any person that finds her attractive. Like the hostage adapting to her captor's threats, and the employee accommodating abuse from her employer, cultures adapt to inhumane body-image ideals as these body types seem to indirectly support all three hierarchies of need. Like "Corporate Stockholm Syndrome," if all of survival hinges on a person being accepted by achieving a body image that requires she diet, it would make sense that she'd have the abnormal condition of a *Body-Diet Supremacy Syndrome*.

In cultures where thin(ner) supremacy is a widely accepted body image, followers are expected to watch their weight, measure their bodies, and perpetually find ways to restrict their needs and urges for food. Unfortunately, dieting and excessive exercise for the sake of being accepted would put a huge population of people (particularly females) at high risk of this psychological phenomenon.

In effect, believers are put into a position to restrict food and restrict their body, as a means to receive validation from others, and in fear of social ridicule and rejection. Followers who don't meet the ideal standards must do whatever it takes, even if its inhumane…because it's "for their own good." Otherwise they stand the risk of being publicly judged, demoted to a lower social status, and seen as sickly human beings. The same attitude applies to groups where health-supremacy body image beliefs require radical food restrictions or other methods like exercise. As described in the previous chapters, idealized dieting and exercise methods have their own narcissistic image.

Diet and exercise images are commonly encouraged as honorable symbols of superiority, but are also methods of punishment—proselytized as what a person needs to do in order to improve him or herself.

Many of the clients I've worked with refused to actually live their life because they believed their body wasn't worthy…yet.

- Their fear of rejection was so intense that they held themselves hostage in their home, believing the narcissistic dogma that they weren't worthy of love, companionship, or even going out in public.

- The only freedom they gave themselves was through a thinner body image—believing they didn't deserve food, social engagement, or basic needs like clothes and intimacy, until they achieved a thinner or healthier body.

- Anxiety about the "health" of food, and being seen eating something deemed "bad" or unhealthy, paralyzed their desire to eat publicly.

- Narcissistic ideologies of thin(ner) and/or health(ier) supremacy, combined with diet and exercise images they internalized as truth, hold them captive—not only controlling their value to society, but also the relationship they have with their body, and their access to food.

Over a lifetime of being strictly held to such inhumane expectations in order to earn someone else's approval, as if disapproval is like having a gun pointed at your head, it wouldn't be surprising when dogmatic and more perfectionistic followers showed signs and symptoms of "Complex" Post-traumatic Stress Disorder (Complex PTSD).

Complex Post-traumatic Stress Disorder (CPTSD)

"People who have experienced severe aversive events while under the totalitarian control of other people are likely to experience mental death, a loss of the identity that they had prior to their interpersonal trauma." [23]

– Angela Ebert, PhD, et al., Published scientists studying Complex PTSD

When people think of Post-traumatic Stress Disorder (PTSD), they typically think of someone who has been traumatized by a specific dangerous and death-defining event, or a grouping of traumatizing events. The American Psychiatric Association defines PTSD as "the development of characteristic symptoms following a psychologically distressing event that is outside the range of usual human experience…The stressor producing this syndrome would be markedly distressing to almost anyone."

People don't necessarily consider that PTSD *could occur because of trauma in relationships.* According to Judith Lewis Herman, psychiatrist and researcher at the Harvard University Medical School: Complex PTSD is a proposed syndrome in survivors of prolonged and repeated trauma that can occur only where the victim is in a state of captivity, and under the control of the perpetrator.[22] The psychological effect of being manipulated and controlled by an authority has many common features, whether it occurs in public through politics or in private like sexual and domestic relations.[22]

Complex PTSD, or complex trauma syndrome, can be seen in people who've experienced prolonged totalitarian control that causes symptoms that are severe, complex, and more enduring. Unlike PTSD, complex PTSD impacts a person's identity and can be so traumatic over time that it causes "mental death," which is a loss of their personal self-concept that existed prior to their interpersonal trauma.[23]

Symptoms of complex PTSD arise from threats to psychological integrity rather than physical. According to scientists Angela Ebert and Murray J. Dyke, symptoms of mental death are:

- Guilt and shame about oneself,

- Distrust and alienation from others,

- Loss of personal independence and autonomy,

- Loss of core beliefs and values, and

- A sense of being permanently and irreparably damaged.

When there's been a total loss of personal self, escaping an enslaved mind feels like suicide. These are symptoms that I have experienced, as well as observed in many of the clients I've worked with who suffered with an eating disorder.

> **When your entire self-concept has been stifled and repressed by totalitarian body and diet image control—escaping that life can feel as if you're dying or that you're giving up your only sense of purpose, safety, and existence.**

This is particularly true for people who've leaned on narcissistic body and diet images to cope in self-defense from traumatic interpersonal events. This is the basis for the third possible condition I believe might contribute to more severe outcomes of an eating disorder as a Body-Diet Supremacy Syndrome. Here is a reminder of the third point I've included as part of the syndrome:

3. *Traumatic interpersonal experience that would lead to shame-based self-soothing, punishment, and other coping mechanisms used to hide from or fight internalized stigma and fears of rejection and abandonment.*

I assume the most severe cases of people suffering with an eating disorder have an increased level of complex PTSD. In these cases, stopping the eating disorder behaviors would expose a person's trauma, and would open him or her up to feelings of terror. Letting go of the abusive body- and diet-image that their entire identity and devotion in life is molded around, would feel like suicide.

That devotion provides a distraction and a way to fight and protect oneself from illusions that he or she might have flaws or a weakness that might have attracted the trauma. Of course, this thought isn't true, but in order to protect oneself from reexperiencing trauma, it makes sense that she'd look within herself to find a fault so she can work on herself, in order to prevent the trauma from happening again. For this reason, people who have been traumatized might search for a strong external fix that would give them black-and-white boundaries, measures, and strict rules to "fix" who they are and to protect them from their "bad" and vulnerable selves. Authoritarian-style religions, politics, and beliefs (like narcissistic body-image beliefs), would be the perfect match for their internal sense of badness, guilt, and shame that might attract further trauma.

Without a totalitarian or authoritarian-style belief system to cover everything up and provide rules and regulations as a means to fight and distract from trauma, life can seem like a vast space of infinite vulnerability to continued terror. It seems safer to stick to the familiar darkness and isolating misery you know than to go into a space of unknown freedom you don't understand and can't predict. People don't realize they are killing themselves—the more they devote their identity to the narcissistic body and diet-image belief systems thinking—that's how they will survive trauma.

Request for my help from a woman in her mid-60s:
I have been struggling with Binge Eating Disorder, bulimia, anorexia, and obesity for over 30 years. I've had gastric banding, tried every diet under the sun (I could have a PhD in dieting), have always obsessed about food, diet, weight, and exercise for all of my adult life. I have been in Inpatient, Residential and Outpatient Therapy for over 10 years. I have periods of recovery, but nothing that has lasted. I struggle to get past the fact that I have to accept my weight, even if it isn't healthy. It feels like I can't escape needing to diet because I believe that if I can lose weight, I can have both recovery and health.

I'm afraid of what life would be like if I didn't need to work on my body because my entire life has been about my weight. I don't know who I'd be if I were to let this all go. You are the only person I've found that makes sense, and I'm hoping you'd be willing to help me.

Killing Yourself to Survive

When I read descriptions of how a person gets entranced to stay in such horrifically abusive situations, my mouth dropped. The combination of things that are found in people with these issues, described both how I felt and the facets that created the space of my eating disorder.

Think of it this way: approval or disapproval from your leader has sole power and control over determining your access to food, water, shelter, and basically your first and second hierarchy of needs. Approval equates to safety and relief, and disapproval equates to punishment and the danger of hunger, isolation, and abuse. *Wouldn't you do what you're told in order to survive?*

What impels people to stay in abusive and dangerous relationships when they have the means and opportunity to escape, is 1) when they don't have a sense of ability to survive on their own, and 2) when they internalize and agree with the authority's ideas and beliefs that determine the process by which they earn inclusion and reward, or exclusion and punishment. In cultural settings, typically people believe ideas and fantasies of what life should be like, which determines the rules and restrictions that they reinforce within themselves and for others to live by.

When cruelty is accepted as necessary, and fear is used to move people into compliance, believers don't need others to threaten the rules when they're willing to do it to themselves—"for their own good."

When I put together the cultures of thin and health supremacy as the grandiose narcissistic authority, and dogmatic beliefs about restricting food as the rules and regulations that make a person worthy of love and acceptance, to me it looks like a form of Stockholm Syndrome. What has solidified my connection to eating disorders as a possible dual-survival syndrome are descriptions of what it takes for a person to escape.

This is exactly what I experienced when I escaped from the dark space of my eating disorder:

- **The dissolution of the fantasy,**

- **Seeing the truth about the cruelty,**

- **Accepting loss of inclusion,**

- **Accepting the vulnerability of exclusion, and**

- **Voluntarily making the coherent choice to leave, with instantaneous and permanent relief.**

What makes this difficult for many people to see, is that body or diet images aren't a defined and named community, leader, or person. To recover, a person isn't escaping an abusive person, or religious cult—she's leaving a radicalized diet, fitness, and health industry. She's freeing herself from taking seriously the rules and controls that are being promoted everywhere, which don't necessarily have a name or identity.

It would be easier for people to recognize this syndrome if those that suffered were showing signs of misery from inside a defined totalitarian religious or political group. This is why it is so helpful to think about it in terms of "thin(ner) supremacy" or narcissistic body-image supremacy. It's a grandiose belief system that defines what you have to do to earn approval and inclusion, but what makes it more intense is that they also strictly instruct how, when, and what can and cannot be eaten.

I suspect, with a different body image that doesn't demonize body fat or regulate access to food, this syndrome wouldn't arise the same way or be so difficult to escape. When it involves access to food, it would most definitely seem as though noncompliance would be a life-and-death situation.

> **IMPORTANT:** When narcissistic ideology is given authoritarian control over a culture's identity and determines what's acceptable or not, it would make sense that dogmatic believers would show signs and symptoms of vulnerable narcissism as they strive to assimilate in order to blend in and be included. When reaching that identity also dictate how people should eat and what authorizes access to food, while using fear, judgment, and shame to motivate compliance, not following the rules would feel as if you're doing something wrong, and *might have a terrorizing impact.*

If being seen negatively has a terrorizing impact, it would make sense that the survival energy of the first (food) and second hierarchies of need (safety in your environment/surroundings/life) would combine to support whatever it takes to "fit in." Ultimately, the self-destructive behavior of people clutching to their abusive eating behavior as a way to remove that terror, seems reasonable when it's looked at from the vantage point of a person experiencing the phenomenon of Stockholm Syndrome, or trauma bonding. For me, when my experience of an eating disorder is applied as a syndrome, the suffering I endured, and my miraculous escape and recovery makes complete sense.

Request to work with me from a woman in her late 30's:

I am desperate for help. I am 37 and have been on a diet or in binge mode literally since the second grade. I have been in so many programs I can't even count them. I have been diagnosed with OCD, Bulimia and Binge Eating Disorder. I have weighed from 130 pounds to 320 pounds and everywhere in between. Right now, I am currently gaining and am 225 pounds, and I am 5'7. I don't know what to do. I can't afford $40,000 to go into an in-patient treatment center. Also, I am getting a lot of reactions such as ...since I am not too thin, I am not really sick. WHAT THE HELL! I am at the end of my rope, and I think it was not an accident that I found your videos online.

Chapter 8

Superior Syndrome—When Narcissistic Body and Diet Images Combine

"The food, diet, and fitness industries, aided by the media, espouse the message that independence for women in general, means self-improvement, self-control, and that it is the women's responsibility to achieve the ultra-slender body ideal; while the converse of this connotes laziness, indignity, self-indulgence, lack of control, and moral failure. The family peer group and school often mirror and

amplify these messages, which often take the form of rewards and punishments that urge women's bodies toward slenderness…If you work hard, you will be rewarded; as if thinness is achievable to all women who strive for it."

– Sharlene Hesse-Biber, et al. 2006, *The Mass Marketing of Disordered Eating and Eating Disorders; The Social Psychology of Women, Thinness, and Culture*

Narcissistic Body and Diet Images

Of the five conditions I believe attribute to the combined outcome of an eating disorder as a syndrome, the last two will be discussed in this chapter. I believe the first three conditions described in previous chapters are precursors to a person being attracted to and seeking out narcissistic belief systems as a way to survive. As a reminder, here or those conditions:

1. Large abundance and wealth of food that insulates a society from the risk and awareness of environmental famine and uncontrollable starvation.

2. A personal position of needing external validation from others to secure his or her third hierarchy of need: to feel worthy of love, inclusion, and acceptance.

3. Traumatic interpersonal experience that would lead to shame-based self-soothing, punishment, and other coping mechanisms used to hide from or fight internalized stigma and fears of rejection and abandonment.

The two conditions discussed in this chapter are specific to the belief systems that I believe intertwine and define the syndrome: narcissistic body and diet images. As a reminder, here are those conditions:

4. Identifying primarily, or more heavily by narcissistic body images as a means to secure one's third hierarchy of need to earn love, inclusion, and acceptance.

 – A form of measurement is needed to compare her body to the ideal image, i.e., circumference measurements, weight, body-fat percentages, clothing size, visual cues like hip bones, ribs, collar bones, or thigh gaps. This might include measurements such as burned calories, resting metabolic rates, resting heart rate, blood pressure, etc. With concepts of "health" that can't necessarily be measured, people use some form of measurable supply, like an organized diet or exercise routine. This is the next condition attributing to the syndrome.

5. Identifying primarily, or more heavily by narcissistic "diet images" as a means to supply measurement and controls for a superior body image. Food restriction necessitates additional support, strictness, isolation, controls and measurements to repress increased urges to eat as one's first hierarchy of need is triggered as insecure.

 – This includes one or more means of control, like the promise of continued and more strict dieting after eating is allowed, narcissistic exercise images, diuretic abuse, purging, chewing and spitting out food, appetite suppressants, nutritional supplementation abuse, etc.

Gambling with the Indirect Probability That You'll Survive

When Dr. Abraham Maslow suggested humans have priorities when it comes to survival, I believe he was accurate when he placed the motivation *to feel worthy of love and belonging as a third-level priority*. However, if the

157

power to secure your third hierarchy of need is defined by grandiose narcissists who threaten judgment, ridicule, and rejection if you aren't thinner or healthier—*the first and most important hierarchy of need to feel secure with food would be challenged.*

When a person adapts to this idea, and believes she isn't worthy of love and inclusion because she thinks she isn't healthy or thin enough, eating becomes a direct threat to her inner instinct and yearning to "fit in." Survival mechanisms and energy meant to aid the ability to blend in and adapt to culture are harnessed toward blending in with a diet that fights food *as a common enemy.* From this position it seems as if dieting is a good thing, like a righteous defense weapon, or a narcissistic supply that provides a person the benefit of inclusion into a diet community.

Like a game of probability, depriving oneself of the most vital life needs in order to secure acceptance from other people is a gamble between competing survival mechanisms.

Our chances of survival improve significantly when we safely belong in a pack or group of people because inclusion increases the likelihood that you'll have access to the most important direct and vital needs of food, water, and shelter. In a sense, if you don't believe you can survive on your own, the drive for physiological and environmental requirements projects and harnesses energy toward relationships with others as if their inclusion is the most important need—predominantly if they have access to food, water, and shelter in abundance.

This makes it seem as if others' approval and acceptance is a direct and vital need. But the truth is, it's not. Belonging to a group is an indirect need that might improve the probability that your vital needs will be secured. It's not a guarantee. However, it can seem like less of a gamble if believers follow the dogmatic rules and concepts with painstaking perfectionism. The illusion is that your survival depends on your strict compliance, and that perfectionism applied to food restrictions has survival-oriented consequences. When being accepted demands that you voluntarily threaten access to food, *the indirect means to secure life becomes a direct factual threat to life.*

Looking at it from a distance, this is a sick form of torture that's culturally being worshipped and sold as superior and "healthy."

Because food is needed to sustain life, expecting someone to radically restrict eating just to be liked and included—is obviously inhumane and horribly abusive. This is like advocating that people restrict sleeping, going to the bathroom, or drinking water in a competition of self-restraint and control over the body's survival needs—to prove who has the most value. When the majority can't meet the restrictive standards, they're deemed inadequate, and are treated as if they're inferior people who can't handle it and who don't want it enough. Winners are given a pedestal of honor, but must continue to live in restraint to maintain their higher status.

Consider the cruelty—expecting people to restrict food like they're in a poverty-stricken environment while living in abundance and surrounded by others who have full access to food. When body fat is stigmatized and disgraced, it makes sense that believers would think forced-food restriction is the right thing to do. Like body-image supremacy, this encourages diet-image supremacy.

Not only is a person to uphold a "lifestyle image," but that image is used as narcissistic supply to a superior body image. In effect, narcissistic survival of the third hierarchy of need holds the first hierarchy of need captive to perform above and beyond what is sanely possible.

Promoting a diet "lifestyle" to attain a superior body image in order to feel safe and accepted in society is terribly problematic.

The Narcissistic Supply of "Diet Image" and Food Restrictions

The idea that being thinner is healthier doesn't include the psychological impact on how people are driven to eat in order to stay alive.

From this vantage point, it isn't surprising when dieters tend to struggle with "emotional eating." This is extremely difficult for people to see because overeating is judged and shamed as a lack of willpower and a sign of a person's flawed character, rather than being looked at as a natural reaction that's triggered when a person's survival mechanisms are urging him or her to do.

When overeating is shamed and people look at it in disgust, undereating is equally emphasized as a symbol of superiority. Therefore, not only is thinness worshipped, but so is the ability to repress the increasing urges to eat. Like a body image, standards of a diet image are put in place by some authoritarian dogma.

Weight-loss businesses will tell you 1) exactly what, when, and how you can and cannot eat or drink, 2) what water alkalinity is best, 3) what time to exercise, 4) what exercise is best, 5) when to sleep, 6) what your heart rate should be, 7) how many calories you need to burn, etc.

The superior "diet image" becomes a form of narcissistic supply to the underlying health- or thin-supremacy body image it serves.

Unfortunately, this encourages people to isolate themselves in order to curb and control the natural increase in desire to eat that occurs as a result of forced-food restriction. For people who are privileged enough to be able to remove themselves from reality, this has its own set of unintended consequences.

If given the ability to isolate oneself so that eating isn't an option, not only will a person feel euphoria about successfully attaining the body image she fantasized would symbolize her worth, but she is gratified by the ability to control the animal nature impelling her to eat. She has gained an attached sense of personal accomplishment and pride for being able to overpower hunger.

MY EXERIENCE: *I recall feeling a wave of positive emotions when I was able to overcome and sit through hunger pains and my desires to eat. It was like winning a war or battle that proved I was capable of something difficult. I had defeated my own body, and this felt incredibly powerful. However, this required I isolate myself from temptation, which wasn't always an option. I was on scholarship to play volleyball at the university I was attending, taking classes, and having to go to the store for myself. When there were team dinners, I was forced to be around the sights and smells of food I couldn't avoid. Ordering from a menu was a direct threat to my pride and sense of ability to hide from my survival impulses to eat.*

The more I was forced to interact with people around food, the less control I had, and the more I ended up binge eating mass quantities of food. Eventually, in order to remove shame for not being able to contain myself and as a way to regain feelings of success and pride, I resorted to puking up food, plus I added extreme exercise. Had I been in an environment where I didn't have to eat with others, go out in public to restaurants or the grocery store, or have to physically perform for a highly powerful sport, I would have been more successful in my anorexic endeavors. I contend, bulimia for me was the only way to function as an "anorexic" when I was required to function around food and people in real life.

I have vivid recollection of the anger and rage I directed at anyone who got in the way of my ability to restrict food, or binge and purge. Without my ability to control it all, I felt like a caged animal fight-

ing to get out. I'd do anything, even if it meant stealing from my parents, exercising in the middle of the night, or faking that I was drunk so I could puke up the food in order to maintain my sense of value and to feel safe again. Anyone or thing that got in the way of my ability to diet, binge, or purge were direct threats to my survival. They were my enemy. I knew I was treating loved ones terribly, but I didn't know how to stop, especially when they were trying to "help" me. They didn't know it, but they were trying to take away the only things I knew to do to survive. They were threatening my narcissistic supply—and the only way I felt good about myself.

When your value is defined by narcissistic body images of thinness, the ability to refrain from food can feel empowering and become your only sense of value and pride. Having to socialize becomes a direct threat to feeling good about yourself. Your parents, friends, and coworkers become an irritating obstruction to your sense of success and value because of their demands and wanting to sit down and eat with you. When you can't maintain perfect success, the slightest deviation feels as if it has ruined any hope for the day, and the urge to can be overwhelming.

> **NOTE:** For a binge eater, being withheld from food can agitate a deep anger that will fight for a way to eat forbidden food. If given the opportunity to be alone, you will consume mass quantities of food, and will experience a sense of freedom. But soon after, shame for not being able to control yourself comes up, fear of damage done to your body and health takes over, and the need to diet doesn't seem negotiable. This person does not only have a negative body image, but also a negative diet image.

For me, when I thought all hope for dieting success had been ruined, I would feel an incredible surge of excitement and euphoria as freedom to eat without shame, guilt, or restraint was a possibility. However, this freedom was made possible only when I committed to fix the damages of that binge, by puking up the food, over-exercising, and returning to food restriction with even more vigilance. Anybody that got in the way of my freedom to binge or who threatened my ability to diet or purge, I treated with anger and rage.

You could say that bulimia is how a person who seeks inclusion through a thin(ner)-supremacy body image maintains the safety of her status, when she can't control neither her exposure to food or the raging need to eat that occurs as a consequence. She's trying to maintain her diet image, when urges to eat are too strong, in order to maintain her body image. For believers who are struggling to manage both, the degree of shame and the intensity of strictness they hold themselves to only goes up. This predisposes them to binge cycles that result in more weight gain, more anxiety around food, stricter dieting, and more bingeing.

The Diet-Binge-Diet Cycle

Imagine setting out to lose weight in order to feel better about your body. To reach the desirable image in your mind, it will take sustained food restriction and degrees of starvation, all while being surrounded by the food you aren't supposed to eat. Each and every time you restrict food for extended periods of time, your body might lose fat, however:

- Your mind fixates on and magnifies interest in the food you can't eat,

- Your hunger for that food gets bigger and more appetizing, and

- Restricting that food increasingly becomes psychologically agitating and straining. Eventually the desire and need for food surpasses the desire to be thinner, and the urge to eat grows beyond the limits of the diet.

- Your desire to eat negotiates for lenience in the diet, but the stricter and more perfectionistic it is, the more likely you are to falter and overeat.

- Minor mistakes feel catastrophic to your weight-loss goals when you're walking on the eggshells of a strict diet, and

- When you believe the extra eating has ruined your chances of losing weight, there's no perceived benefit to continuing the strain and agitation of restriction.

In addition, once you commit to "getting back on track" afterwards in order to fix everything, there's space and time to 1) indulge without having to gingerly tiptoe around food, and 2) to not feel bad or ashamed about gaining weight. These two freedoms feel incredibly liberating and euphoric, but only temporarily. When the bingeing is all done, the shame and fear about weight gain returns, and so does increasing pressure to restrict perfectly. I describe this all-or-nothing pendulum swing between the pressure to under-eat and resultant overeating as the *diet-binge-diet cycle.*

The diet-binge-diet cycle starts with a diet—that when failed, ends in a binge. That binge is enabled by the commitment to another diet, as if it's guaranteed the next diet will rescue you and fix the harm that bingeing does. Although, for most people the diet never truly fixes anything—especially when the strictness and perfectionism of it cracks under very little pressure from eating one or two failed bites of food.

Eventually, people end up eating more and more with longer periods of time between diets, thinking the weight gain will eventually get fixed by the next anticipated diet. The thinner look you originally set out to achieve becomes more and more distant. Consequently, there's a significantly larger impulsive need to eat in anticipation for a longer and more severe famine. You can read a more thorough description about the impulse to overeat and binge in section 2 of *Diet Supremacy*.

Using Fear of Unhealth to Motivate Compliance

One technique diet images use to encourage people from eating is to demonize food as "unhealthy" or toxic. The idea is that "health" will be a more inspiring and meaningful diet image for people to subscribe to in order to motivate food restriction when trying to reach an ideal body image.

Shaming and judging food as "toxic" and "bad" make the rules around restrictions of the diet image more distinct for people to understand and control in public, especially if food restrictions are seen as the morally "right" thing to do. An illusion is created that makes it seem as if people who eat freely are in danger, and the people who follow the "correct" food rules are safe from threat.

This is a shield that seems to maintain a person's superior health status, and justifies radical eating restrictions that otherwise would make him or her stand out in public as bizarre.

This would make sense for why people in "healthy supremacy" would struggle to contain themselves from talking in public about 1) how horrible and toxic food is, 2) how disgusted they are about people who don't seem to care, and 3) why everyone should refrain from unhealthy food. This anger and rage against food is a way to protect their diet image and to insulate themselves from temptation. This image protects them from being exposed as insecure with themselves, their body, and food. It's easier to position oneself as "all knowing" than to admit he or she is probably more scared about being exposed as inferior than they are about being unhealthy.

If motivation was about health, they'd see the downside of paranoia, recognize the need for balance, pleasure, and diversity with food, as well as the importance of eating and sharing a meal with loved ones in peace. For a health supremacist, fear of inferiority projects a diet image onto food, making the choice to eat "good" or "bad" a moral decision, and the dangers of food an all-or-nothing matter. Not only is your body image of health superior, but your ability to refrain from bad food makes you superior.

Email from YouTube follower in her 30's:
Hi Robin, I've been following your YouTube videos for a while and feel as if you're someone I can really talk to. But now I have reached a point in my life where I'm at my wits end. I have battled my weight since I was a teenager. I've never really been skinny, and for a long time I was okay with it. Like you said, those were the years I didn't have issues with food. But about a year ago I decided to do the ketogenic diet, with intermittent fasting, and lost about 35 pounds. But I've lost and regained 20 of those pounds this year too. The reason for this is because I will follow the diet for about a month or two, and then I end up gaining anywhere from 10-15 pounds back because I go on bingeing/purging or just bingeing sprees. So, I eventually get back on wagon and diet strictly to re-lose the weight. I am getting so obsessive over my weight and so emotionally drained from all the dieting that I have now developed an anxiety disorder and have had frequent panic attacks over it.

I feel that I am ALWAYS on a diet and cannot enjoy my life for fear of gaining the weight back. I have avoided social situations where I know there will be food and/or drinking present so instead of enjoying my life, I shut myself in. Other times when I allow myself to indulge, I completely go on an all-out bingeing spree, and I feel horrible about myself shortly after. I used to binge and purge,

166

but now I've gotten past the purging and just end up bingeing and living with the discomfort after. Sometimes I feel as if dieting has been the best and worst thing that ever happened to me. At first it allowed me to lose weight and lose weight quickly. But if I add back in the "normal" foods, it causes me to gain weight so easily that it frustrates me, and then I give up and go back to old eating habits, (bingeing, or just unhealthy eating). I get depressed about the weight I have put back on, and I can't help but to go back to dieting. As I mentioned before, this requires that I avoid going out, which really drains and frustrates me.

Currently I am strictly dieting and losing the weight. I really, really, really, do not want to go into that "dark place" again by bingeing and gaining the weight back and definitely DO NOT want to diet this way anymore. I realize it isn't realistic. But for now, I need to lose the weight. I would really love to have my sanity back again and stop worrying and being so obsessive about gaining weight. I just want to lose weight and be free from thinking about it.

I realize that I have been rambling and I apologize for that, but I feel that you, being experienced with dieting, bingeing, and eating disorders would have more understanding of these kinds of things. Watching your YouTube videos, I often thought to myself, "If only I lived in her area, I would love to have her to talk to. You really seem to 'get it.'"

I understand you must be very busy but I would greatly appreciate any words of advice or even if you have a colleague in your field that you may know or recommend that lives in the Southern California area that I may consult with, preferably with your similar expertise (fat chance I know, but it's worth a shot asking). Any words are greatly and tremendously appreciated.

When Body Image Gets Cultish

The promotion of more radical body images and fear-based diet images has become popularized by "experts" on the internet who more often than not, might suffer from their own superior survival syndrome. I assume they might be grandiose narcissists who seek to have power and receive validation from co-narcissists or vulnerable narcissistic followers. It's not uncommon that leaders in "health" see illness through the eyes of stigma, as they uphold "unhealth" as a moral choice.

Studies of people suffering with disordered eating that looks like orthorexia (an unhealthy obsession of pure and "clean" eating), describe personifying concepts of healthy eating as being sign of righteous morality. As described by Dr. Steven Bratman, the doctor who coined the term:

> *"It (orthorexia) has an aspirational, idealistic, spiritual component which allows it to become deeply rooted in a person's identity. It is most often only a psychological problem in which food concerns become so dominant that other dimensions of life suffer neglect."* [19]

To me, when concepts of "health" get paired with the vanity of being seen as virtuous, this is a clear sign that survival mechanisms are inflamed. Specifically, it is a threat to a person's need for being seen as lovable through narcissistic "health" concepts of body image, but also a threat to the need to feel safe from "dangerous food" through hypervigilant restrictions. My guess is that these people suffer from a combination of two major hierarchies of survival needs being triggered as unsafe at the same time together. For example, if you don't eat healthy, your life will be threatened, your diet image will be negative, and so will your standing and worth in society.

Superior Syndrome—When Narcissistic Body
and Diet Images Combine

People with these types of diet-image and body-image belief systems would be impelled to seek to control and "probe" their food environment with underlying fears of food-danger and death, but also with narcissistic fears of exposure and embarrassment that would occur if they were seen as unhealthy.

> **Their goal of being seen as valuable in their community is using heightened survival mechanisms that seek to feel safe with food as a prideful symbol of supremacy.**

Ultimately, both insecure mechanisms exponentially magnify feelings of danger to the point that believers suffer with obsessive paranoia and hatred of "bad" food, as a shameful symbol of immorality and unhealth. This makes their expectations, rules, and regulations more and more perfectionistic and less and less forgiving.

MY EXPERIENCE: *For me, having high levels of fitness and leanness defined safety with my body, but also the vanity of my desires for inclusion. It was an extreme double-survival insecurity requiring that I perfect both in unison in order to feel secure. In the end, this felt like my survival was cannibalizing my life—or that what kept me alive was killing me.*

From my personal experience with this, it feels like your mind and intellect are held hostage, and you are forced to probe and intellectualize the complexity of food and your body to the point of obsession. I thought that the more information I could learn about metabolism, fitness, fat loss, and nutrition would remove the extreme fear I felt inside. I ended up getting a degree in exercise sci-

ence, and became an "expert" at fat metabolism. This gave my survival mechanisms a direction to work, through the illusion that with knowledge, I could control vulnerability. I was driven to insulate myself from being exposed by gleaning as much knowledge as possible to detect danger more easily.

This type of dual-image survival can occur with other body images, like bodybuilding, sexuality, beauty, or fitness. In terms of anorexia, this would be like gaining the pride of thin(ner) supremacy through the pride of starvation too. In other words, your needs to "fit in" are holding your needs for food hostage, *in pride.* To someone in this state of mind, eating would feel like death, and so would body fat. Sadly—without both—death is guaranteed.

Like a religious cult leader, sanctimonious experts in health and fitness who suffer this grandiose way, think they are guiding others to the mirage of safety, superiority, and freedom, but in reality they are unconsciously spreading shame and judgments based on information that's been distorted and catastrophized in their mind through projections of radical fear. Devout vulnerable followers end up praising and taking pride in their intense impulses to probe their environment for impurities and "badness," as if life's righteous purpose is to make sure through survival force, that the body is safe from its own dangerous fragility. And others that don't do the same are demeaned as if … *"They just don't get it."*

Believers truly think the sacrifices they make are for their own good, but in the end, they might end up suffering with symptoms of mental illness—thinking they'll be exposed as a loser, and something horrific will happen without their dual narcissistic diet- and body-image survival dogmas to protect them.

This is what anybody would do when their mind is distorted to fight for survival. It's no different than wanting to understand the environment that tigers, bears, and other predators inhabit or might be hiding in. People in this state of mind are doing exactly what survival would request of them under the insecure circumstance. They think that a sense of safety will be accessed through the power of the intellect, which is a mirage.

This is like a very deceptive deal with the devil, as the cost is the freedom of your mind in exchange for an illusion of safety in a controlled "cage" of being. You might be "healthy," but your life is disabled by the slave work needed to sustain this state of the body.

The human mind is closed and dualistic in survival in order for energy to be harnessed toward forcing an end result. In this state of mind, it's very difficult to see relativity and to comprehend the dynamic nature of life. Therefore, the use of intellect to survive is a losing battle due to the biased nature that seeks to secure perceived weakness at all cost. Your intellect is held hostage to fight for the weakest survival link.

Even now, as I use the same survival "probe" in an attempt to intellectualize and understand the elaborate suffering of conflicting survival mechanism as it relates to eating disorders, it's impossible to actually "know" what's really going on. In humility, I contend we as humans aren't capable. We're aren't cerebrally and intellectually as evolved or as smart as our inflated survival ego thinks we are.

Notably in situations where food restrictions that are exalted by health "experts" have the unintended consequence of triggering primal psychological survival mechanisms to defend food consumption at all cost.

IMPORTANT: Survival needs provide safety and pleasure on one hand, but on the other hand, when threatened they trigger fear, perfectionism, paranoia, and obsession. However, in terms of survival, being accepted into a group isn't as vital as having access to food, which would make it incredibly conceited and naive to assume that losing weight to gain approval would be more rewarding than the drive to eat. *Giving diet- and body-image supremacy the power over your third hierarchy of need means that survival mechanisms meant to gain acceptance into your culture are perpetually focused towards endangering your more vital need to feel secure with food.*

As there's an increase in survival focus and energy harnessed toward controlling and diminishing food, primitive animal mechanisms engage that shifts the mind to increase desires and motivations to eat, like a bear preparing for hibernation. Inevitably, without the ability to isolate oneself from food, the growing inner agitation seeking to eat surpasses the smaller, less-important motivation to lose weight.

Once freedom to eat is allowed, the survival mind revels with euphoric satisfaction at gaining access to food in abundance. It feels like a tsunami wave of release from the pressure, tension and strain the diet image imposes on the mind. However, access to food without controls poses a threat to the belief that being thinner and healthier improves your value to your community. The euphoria and freedom to eat is followed by a clashing wave of shame for not being able to control yourself.

The naive idea that restricting food should be easy if you really want to be healthy and lose weight, sets a person up to assume she has character flaws or that she lacks personal capacity when she can't contain her survival urges to eat inside her diet image framework.

As her body gains weight, warning signals sound off that she's at risk of being seen as inferior, inadequate, and worthy of rejection. In the end, she subscribes to restrictive diets that are even more perfectionistic, and she removes herself from social settings "for her own good."

Superior Syndrome—When Narcissistic Body and Diet Images Combine

When a person punishes herself for not being able to restrict food to the degree that diet-image dogma dictates, and shames herself for not being able to fix her body to fit the mold prescribed by the body-image authority, she doesn't need to fear rejection and abandonment from the authority—because she's been *convinced to do it to herself.*

> *"It is the ultimate human paradox that man's dependence on perception precludes his being able to know his own identity."*

– Dr. David R. Hawkins, *The Eye of the I*, page 220

Chapter 9

Trapped Inside Body-Diet Supremacy Syndrome

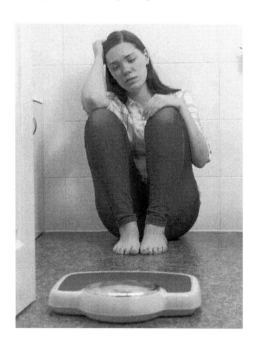

"Ideal beauty is ideal because it does not exist: the action lies in the gap between desire and gratification. Women are not perfect beauties without distance. That space, in the consumer culture, is a lucrative one."

– Naomi Wolf, 1991 author of *The Beauty Myth*

If disordered eating and eating disorders stem from a survival-oriented syndrome like trauma bonding, Societal Stockholm Syndrome, or complex PTSD, the way it is approached as a disorder, addiction or disease might need to be evaluated. This is not to say that disease or an addiction doesn't exist in circumstances where a person is obsessed with food—where she struggles to stop bingeing, or controlling, and wanting to starve herself.

Nonetheless, if the desire for food or to starve yourself is in any way related to shame about body fat, pressure to lose weight, or self-righteous pride attached to being "healthier" or thinner, perhaps the eating disorder isn't a "disorder." Maybe it's a combination of functioning survival-defense mechanisms that function together as protection from narcissistic abuse.

A person that identifies who she is in her mind by the value attached to a healthier or thinner body image will believe dieting is essential as an honorable way for her to belong, be included, or be loved. She has essentially given authority over almost all of her survival needs to be fulfilled by a narcissistic cultural body-image belief system. This would make it a case of "brain washing" or an identity adaptation to an abusive societal belief system, making her obsessions and compulsions about dieting, food, and exercise a symptom of "Societal Stockholm Syndrome." Like getting sucked into a religious cult or a dangerously abusive relationship, she clutches onto her eating disorder as a way to control her survival.

Looking at these issues from this angle makes the odd and dysfunctional behavior of people who have eating disorders *more understandable.* From the spectrum of eating disorders that goes from anorexia and orthorexia, bulimia, and binge eating disorder, what brings a person to survive this way is complicated, and isn't always clear or obvious. However, I am going to attempt to simplify disorders from the viewpoint of a Body-Diet Supremacy Syndrome.

The following descriptions of eating disorders are from the viewpoint of the primary conditions of narcissistic body and diet images. These don't include other aspects I've discussed, like interpersonal trauma such as being molested, assaulted, raised in a religious or political cult, or experiencing long-term abuse in a marriage or family. Clearly, when applying this to people who come from different backgrounds, different levels of trauma, and different cultures, what I've written below would need to be adapted, and it might be completely inappropriate. The goal is to help the reader think about their disordered behaviors from a different perspective, and hopefully that helps open the door to more fully understanding her or her suffering.

It is my intent to present this extremely complex topic of survival as a syndrome in a simple way.

The Case for Binge-Eating Behaviors

> **NOTE:** Both women and men diet, eat emotionally, and suffer from eating disorders. For convenience, I primarily use *she/her* throughout these descriptions.

Binge-eating disorders are complicated in that over time, people develop a co-dependent relationship with eating to cope with stressful life circumstances. I describe this codependency and "addiction" in more detail in section two of *Diet Supremacy.*

Although, without experiencing shame stemming from thin(ner) supremacy ideology and fears of illness threatened by health(ier) supremacy, the urge to demonize food would be less, and the impulse to binge wouldn't be as intense.

For someone with disordered eating behaviors that lean on the side of *binge eating disorder,* she has strong beliefs and experience to show that she is a failure and outcast in thin(ner)- and health(ier)-supremacy cultures. She has failed the system and has abandoned herself in shame and embarrassment from the body-image cult from which she yearns for inclusion.

The more body-image shame she has, the more she:

- Hides herself and excludes herself from life.

- Has constant pressure every waking moment to restrict the foods she's surrounded by.

- Approaches diets and food restrictions with all-or-nothing perfectionism.

- She experiences strain, anxiety, guilt and shame by being around or eating food.

- Will negotiate, reason for, bargain, and justify reasons for eating—*creating an emotional bond with food, as if food rescues her from emotional hardship.*

- Will convince herself that a future diet will fix the fat gain that results from her bingeing.

- Will have euphoria and guiltless "fun" when she gives herself permission to eat, for a short period of time, before she intends to strictly reinforce food restrictions again.

- Feels hopeless and inadequate that she'll ever be loved and included.

- Will believe her health is compromised, no matter what size, weight, or tests that verify she is healthy.

- Will be attracted to radical diet images that moralize and shame food or eating as "dangerous," "bad," and "dirty"— convincing her that being thinner and healthy are possible with their specific diet.

- Believes that dieting is the only way to force her body into "health" and feeling better about herself.

- Will cycle between the pressure to diet and the urge to binge.

Like the outcast seeking to prove her worth and to be received back into her culture, the constant pressure to starve herself overwhelms the primitive mechanism to "feast before" and "feast after" famine as if she will die of starvation otherwise. The same pressure exists for people who suffer from disordered eating that mimics "bulimic" tendencies.

The Case for Bulimic Behaviors

A person that seems to have been included into the culture of thin(ner) supremacy because she's lost weight, might feel vulnerable to losing her approval. This vulnerability comes from a sense of weakness stemming from growing impulses to eat. These urges to eat threaten the body image she's attached her security to. If she can't manage the overwhelming impulses to binge, the only way to defend her body-image safety is to *immediately* remove the vulnerability of weight gain. She has the same exact points listed above that a binge eater experiences. In addition, she experiences:

- Paranoia that she is gaining body fat.

- Constant need to body check, measure her body, and check her weight.

- All-or-nothing failure with slight deviations from her diet plan.

- Commitment to some form of "purging" prior to allowing herself to "lose control" with a binge.

- Euphoria and freedom experienced with the rush of excitement that comes with bingeing.

- Immediate feelings of "fatness" directly after the binge.

- Intense threats of danger and harm attached to that sense of "fatness" after a binge.

- Feelings of death and doom if she doesn't *immediately* respond to the threats of danger as quickly as possible, no matter where she is or how inconvenient the situation.

- The radical urge to instantly resolve weight gain before it happens, unlike a binge eater who commits to fixing her weight *sometime in the future.*

- The impulse to rid the dangerous feelings of "fatness" by puking up eaten food, use diuretics to force the body to expel the food as quickly as possible, exercise to burn off the energy of the food she just ate, or to spit her food out quickly after she chews it.

- Euphoria, safety, and calm after "purging" the fears and feelings of fatness from her body.

Like a person who suffers from binge-eating behaviors, a person who immediately purges when she binges has constant

pressure to restrict, as well as feelings of anxiety and fear of food.

The only difference in her mind is the internal survival-mode death threats that make it seem cataclysmic if she doesn't immediately prevent the risk of fat gain. Dieting isn't a sufficient instantaneous shield from fat gain after a binge, therefore if she doesn't purge, it is guaranteed she will gain body fat. This means she will lose her standing as a thinner person, and will be exposed as a liar and a fraud in the thin(ner)-supremacy community where she wants to "fit in."

Her inability to sustain dieting long enough without bingeing has a lot to do with her inability to isolate herself from temptation, or from being seen as weird, or exposed as anorexic. Many people who have bulimic tendencies are actually anorexic and are trying to be "normal." However, when they cannot hide themselves from food because they want to go back to school, need to get a job, or want to date, the natural urges to eat grow and are very difficult to repress—especially when food restrictions seem "weird." In order to maintain her thinness, and also function socially, her food-restrictive lifestyle will need to be able to handle extreme access to large abundance of food when she's out publicly.

Bulimic Purging: If she struggles to handle the primitive urges that awaken with the sight and smells of food, and the pressure to eat so that she seems "normal"…

- Purging becomes a shield that gives her the freedom to eat, without the risk of fat gain.

- When following the rules of her diet image isn't realistic or possible in social settings, many people attempt to defend their thin(ner) supremacy status by leaning on purging or extreme exercise.

- To someone who is well protected, and can conveniently restrict, her thinness and starvation can become an achievement that defines her.

Anorexia gives her a sense that she is independently succeeding at proving her worth, and that she has something of value that no one else can take from her. She holds herself hostage to her own radical expectations, and her success and slavery to it *becomes her only sense of survival.*

The Case for Anorexic Starvation

Unlike someone struggling with binge eating who is hiding in shame from the stigma of her body, or a person with *bulimia* who is paranoid she'll gain weight and be exposed as an imposter, an *anorexic person* is safe in her cage of thinness and isolation away from food.

An anorexic person:

- Isolates and removes herself from temptation or from anything that challenges her ability to restrict food.

- Knows that having control of the urges to eat is the only way she feels strength, capacity, and safety—to the point where risks associated with emaciation don't matter.

- Feels euphoric and powerful, as if she's defeating weakness and vulnerability, when she refuses food.

- Believes that controlling food and her body gives her autonomy and personal success in her life, commonly when she's been a servant to meeting others' demands.

- Believes that the potential of dying isn't as scary as losing her identity and the only sense of success she's established and understands within her ability to overcome hunger and maintain her thinness.

It doesn't matter if this requires that she remove herself from life, relationships, or family—being able to control the urges to eat, as well as the ultra-thinness used as a symbol of this strength, becomes how she identifies "who she is" and what gives her life purpose. To her, giving that up would feel as if she is committing suicide, despite the fact that she is already gambling with death because of complications due to starvation.

She is literally holding herself hostage, using starvation as proof—and her emaciated body as evidence that she has control and power over what defines who she is and what makes her life safe and worth living. However, the truth is that she isn't using her own definition of worth, but she has internalized the belief system of thin(ner) supremacy, as if it is her own. It gives her the illusion it is her choice, when in reality she is being manipulated by a body-image dogma that promotes the narcissistic ideology that her ability to control her food and body is a sign that her life is worth living. She's achieved this to the most unforgiving, perfectionist, and radical degree. By having this "personal" definition of approval and inclusion, is seems as if the person has totalitarian control over the risk of abandonment, rejection, and disapproval.

In essence, anorexia is a rejection of freedoms in life because freedom is seen as too dangerous and exposing when compared to the cocoon of safety that's been attached to restricting food as a sacrifice that's required by her body image.

Similar to radical cult religions that proselytize "free will" by obeying fear-based commandments to placate a vengeful God, anorexia demands extreme starvation, and also worships the ability to suppress and control primitive urges to eat, as a way to support and comply to the radical narcissistic concept of thin(ner) supremacy.

Like an abused person perceives safety through being compliant to an abuser, a person with anorexia obeys demands of starvation *as if it is her only hope to feel safe* with a body that threatens her life if it isn't thin enough. To stop dieting and to allow her body to gain fat would expose a huge void of emptiness and worthlessness that she's desperately trying to hide from and escape. She would rather die than face that darkness because it seems as if that void will completely decimate her existence. Without starvation and thin supremacy holding her captive, it feels like her entire sense of life will disappear, as if her entire existence will be crushed into dust, and blown away in the wind.

The Case for Narcissistic Orthorexia and Healthy Diet-Image Supremacy

Orthorexia is similar to anorexia; however, it isn't starvation and emaciation that provides a sense of safety. It is the complete and total removal from "unhealthy" foods that supplies her sense of supremacy. In this case, the body image being worshiped isn't thin(ner) supremacy, but it is an image of "healthy supremacy." Although it's common that anorexia, bulimia, and orthorexia go hand in hand, a person who suffers this way doesn't necessarily care about his or her body fat the same way an anorexic would. They are more forgiving of body fat than they are of food that's perceived as unhealthy.

The distinguished health of the food she eats, and her knowledge about food, becomes how she proves her worth and how she values herself and others. Healthy eating can become her entire identity as a person, like a religious zealot who preaches her food controls and beliefs as if it is a moral decision that defines your worth as a human. Her goal is to convert as many people as possible to her healthy and morally right way of eating—and she shames, degrades, and is disgusted by people who don't care about the food they eat the same way she does.

The pride attached to her obsession about what's in the food, who made it, and her ability to control every ingredient and where it is sourced becomes so important that she stops socializing, won't go out to eat, and if she does go out to eat, she brings her own food—even when it seems inappropriate or bizarre.

As the list of foods she allows herself to eat gets smaller and smaller, she ends up with nutritional deficiencies and illness because she isn't supplying adequate nourishment to support her immune system.

Her survival obsession, fixation, and paranoia of unhealthy food might give her a sense of superiority and safety, but she ultimately sabotages relationships because of her judgmental shaming of other's eating habits, and she ends up unhealthier than her supreme diet would have predicted. Typically, instead of looking at her strict removal of "unhealthy" food as the problem, she tries to blame a different ingredient in the food, an environmental factor, or she blames the one time she let herself eat something "bad" as to why her health is chronically suffering. Instead of adding food, she's more likely to restrict more and believe nutritional supplements are the answer. As she continues to worship and devote herself to "healthy eating," like the other body image induced eating disorders—her entire life is held hostage and her mind is entirely devoted to a body image that defines who she is—as if her "healthy" survival depends on it.

Killing Yourself to Belong

In these types of eating disorders, I question if they'd exist without:

1. Interpersonal trauma that would direct a person to internalize herself as inadequate,

2. The survival-oriented coping mechanism to seek external validation to secure her sense of value and worth,

3. The cultural acceptance of narcissistic body and diet images to supply that validation, and

4. The radical abundance and privilege that allows for restrictive diet images to act as narcissistic supply to those body images.

Without understanding how these conditions relate to each other as either the hero or adversary, and what they represent, it's easy for people to assume that eating disorders are simply an addiction about control and food.

But when those who suffer aren't oriented to see the big picture from the outside, it's very difficult to explain or describe what the eating disorder is all about. For me, one of the hardest parts of having an eating disorder was the fact that *I couldn't see why* my desire to control food, and also to exercise excessively, was a life-and-death matter. Despite the fact that these behaviors brought severe suffering, isolation, and misery, I believed my identity and life depended on perfectionistic dieting and exercise as my shield and weapon used to to maintain the body image I was hiding behind.

In this emotional space it feels impossible to escape, especially when there's terrorizing fears of death that seem far worse than the damages being done by the obsessive-compulsive behaviors that protect and keep your mind safe.

Think of it this way, and ask yourself these questions:

- If bingeing stops the feelings that you're going to be starved to death, would you do it?

- If puking food up after you eat excessively gets rid of the feeling that you're going to get pushed off a cliff and fall to your death, would you puke?

- If exercising until complete exhaustion was the only way to experience a sense of peace and calm, would you do it?

- If micromanaging food is the only activity that gives you a sense of success, safety, and purpose, would you do it?

- If bingeing represses and hides feelings of embarrassment, shame, and social anxiety, would you do it?

Many people who don't have an eating disorder or who've never suffered to that degree, don't understand why a person would be so attached to behaviors that cause such incredible harm. What they don't realize is that their loved one who suffers from this type of behavior is doing so because *it's what she thinks she needs to do to stay alive.*

Bingeing, puking, starving, hiding, isolating, cutting yourself, drug abuse, gambling, sexual promiscuity, and anything else she can't seem to impulsively control, is what she feels is necessary to survive.

> **Even if she must lie, steal, hide, and act out abusively, she'll do whatever it takes to continue the self-harming behaviors she believes keep her safe from apparent danger that exists in her mind.**

Like a battered wife, or a person who experiences complex PTSD or trauma bonding, a person suffering with an eating disorder defends her body and diet image despite both resulting in behavior that threatens her body and destroys her life. She ends up threatening her own life while trying to survive. This is like being stuck in a monkey trap.

The Monkey Trap: Because of the perceived benefits, chasing the mirage of thinness with dieting is like being stuck in a monkey trap. This is a trap or cage that has a piece of fruit in it, and when a hungry monkey puts its hand through the hole and grabs the fruit, its newly filled fist becomes too large to exit the cage. He would have to release the fruit in order for his fist to be small enough to get out. If the monkey is not willing to let go of the fruit, he will remain trapped with the fruit in his hand that's stuck in the cage.

The illusion is that the fruit is attainable, and it is, but only to be held and only inside cage. The sustenance, pleasure, and nutrition of the fruit aren't actually available to eat. If the monkey gets entranced by the illusion that it is possible he could eat the fruit he is holding onto, he will devote time, energy, and discomfort on something that is actually impossible. Like chasing a mirage, as the monkey gets hungrier, it becomes more entranced or dependent on the fruit in his hand, keeping him dedicated to something that isn't and will never be edible.

What the monkey thinks is lifesaving is, in fact, life expending, and potentially life-threatening. When he becomes aware that it is impossible to eat it, despite wasting time, life, health, and freedom, he will surrender the mirage of sustenance, let go of the fruit, and set himself free.

Many people who suffer cycling between dieting and emotional eating want to be free from the misery, insanity, and limitation of the trap; however, they also want to keep the prize that continues to keep them in that cage.

In order to escape suffering in the trap of Body-Diet Supremacy Syndrome, clutching to bingeing, dieting, and in isolation, the person must be willing to let go of the safety, protection, and illusions of survival that both body image and diet images supply.

Whatever it is that a person gets out of it, she'd have to give that up if she wants permanent freedom from the darkness and misery being trapped in safety of her survival mechanisms.

Like the monkey letting go of the fruit to gain freedom from the trap, as she surrenders every aspect of the disorder she perceives is important to her survival, she'll inevitably face the terror that appears to threaten her life. Ultimately, she'll have to accept the truth of the outcome in order to escape for good.

For most people, this feels impossible to do. It goes against your evolutionary wiring that demands you should run, fight, hide, and do whatever possible to survive. Without accepting the risk that you might in fact die, you're likely to defend your disordered safety, and fight to stay captive in the syndrome that holds your entire life hostage.

"Darkness cannot drive out darkness; only light can do that. Hate cannot drive out hate; only love can do that."

– Dr. Martin Luther King Jr.

SECTION 4

Accepting Loss, Failure, and Death in Exchange for Freedom

"Your own self-realization is the greatest service you can render the world."

– Ramana Maharshi

Chapter 10

Defending the Disorder
and Fighting to Stay Captive

"What the people in the world actually want is the recognition of who they really are on the highest level, to see that the same Self radiates forth within everyone, heals their feeling of separation, and brings about a feeling of peace. To bring peace and joy to others is the gift of the benevolence of the Presence."

– Dr. David R. Hawkins, *The Eye of the I*, page 91

Request for my help from a woman in her mid 40's:
Dear Robin. I'm 5'6" and weigh 195 pounds. I'm depressed as shit although not a lot of people would guess I was because I'm a happy person. But deep down it's a shitstorm. What's really sad is that I'm a breast cancer survivor for three years now, and I had an easier time accepting cancer than I do being overweight. I'm embarrassed to go out in public and I don't feel like myself. I think you might be the only person I can talk to about this. How do I live life in a body I hate? I feel like I crawled under a rock and am dying. I keep on thinking my only hope is to lose weight, but I can't seem to stick to a diet either. I'm concerned that I'm drinking too much, and I can tell my sanity is slipping. I would like to schedule a consultation as soon as you have an opening. Please, I'm desperate.

Defending the Abuse and Playing the Martyr to Stay with Your Eating Disorder

All of the people who've reached out to me for help I assume struggle from the same survival paradox. There's a sense of safety hidden behind suffering, and many people defend their need to be starved.

In effect, there is something gratifying or hopeful in the struggle to survive. The misery in the work, and the focus that survival requires, gives the illusion there might eventually be a payoff. Because of this, if you guide people to end that struggle and show them the door to escape, many feel loss and become defensive of their suffering.

They experience both feelings of loss and growing anxiety about not knowing what life will be like without the predictability of their miserable existence.

Most people aren't willing to face the reality that maybe they should get help, until they suffer enough and reach complete and total hopeless exhaustion, fatigue, and misery with life dedicated in isolation to the process of dieting and bingeing, and re-dieting and bingeing. In this position it can seem as if it's impossible to escape, and that life can't exist any other way.

This is a critical time for many people, especially if they are considering suicide like I did. But when directed to surrender their eating disorder in order to face the terror that compulsive behavior hides, there is space in that small cage that opens to allow people to escape. They'd have to give up what keeps them safe to intentionally face and accept their biggest fears.

> For people who fear unhealth, they'd have to surrender their diet image and "healthy" behaviors. For someone who is terrified of life stress and the vulnerability judgment and rejection, she'd have to willfully reject food despite the urge to eat as protection, and without expecting weight loss as a reward. Both diet image and body image must be voluntarily and intentionally surrendered, in order to willfully face and accept the originating fear underneath it all.

To start, I direct people to surrender the diet image and "health" behaviors first, because typically these rules and regulations are a form of narcissistic supply to the body image and enable binge-eating behaviors that wouldn't otherwise exist. I suggest they stop all exercise, measuring food, counting calories, and surrendering the morality that defines food as "good" or "bad." It's important that they refuse to use a future diet as a way to escape responsibility for the physical stress that occurs when overeating to cope with life stress.

Refusing the behaviors that shield you from inner feelings of weakness is like ripping the cover off an infected wound to expose the truth of the issues underneath it all.

But if others are wanting you to let the diet image and eating disorder behaviors go before you're ready to face the loss to the body image that lies underneath, those well-meaning people become a source of danger and a threat to your survival-oriented needs because:

- They don't realize, by suggesting you stop bingeing, it seems as if they're wanting you to feel unsafe and exposed emotionally.

- By wanting you to stop over-exercising or puking up your food, it feels as if they are taking away any hope for you to be able to eat without the restraints of a diet.

- By taking away dieting, it appears as if they are threatening the body image you've attached yourself esteem and sense of value to.

To the person suffering, is seems that the people who are helping, are actually hurting you.

Protecting the Body Image by Defending the Diet Image and Disorder

By keeping the diet image, you benefit because it seems as if dieting is the only way to 1) rescue you from feeling out of control with food, 2) remove the weight you've already gained, and 3) protect you from gaining even more weight. However, if you took a step back to look at how dieting has enabled your dysfunctional relationship with food, you'd see that dieting has been a primary source of strain, anxiety, and shame about eating that underlies the emotional charge behind the drive to binge or overeat.

The hardest part of escaping for most people is accepting that to stop binge-ing you'll need to stop dieting, which means you'll have to accept your fears and assumptions that without a diet you'll lose the benefits of your ideal body image.

A person would have to accept her rubbing thighs, her aching knees from extra pounds, and the fear that she might die of every issue/threat that the weight-loss industry uses in order to scare their followers. It's presumed you'll be unhealthy, die early, will never get married, won't have children, your loved ones will abandon you, and you'll be alone forever. The fear thoughts are in-numerable, and those fear thoughts bring about even more fear thoughts, all of which seem like a tsunami wave of death you can't handle. And to make matters more difficult, in cultures that shame and stigmatize body fat, not di-eting means *you have to accept your body* even when you're considered "too big" or not thin enough, and this requires you allow others to judge you and dismiss you as an inferior, insignificant, and lesser human being. This is a direct threat to the entire premise of the underlying superior body image.

In cultures that worship narcissistic body images like thin(ner) supremacy, it seems that losing body fat is the only way you'll feel safe in public, feel good about your life, and be confident in yourself. Therefore, not going on a diet would go against strong survival instincts demanding you do some-thing to protect yourself from being judged and discarded like a piece of trash. These fears come across as truthful and realistic, and when there's an easy way to fix, escape, and repress them, it doesn't make sense to accept them without self-defense.

Refusing the rules and restrictions of a diet image triggers signals of danger that awaken primitive fears of being alone, as if you'll never experience happiness and joy again, or that without a diet your life might as well be over. For this reason, it seems the disorder is impossible to escape.

For many people, letting go of eating disorder behaviors feels as if your life will be irreparably damaged or permanently disfigured—even though the dieting and resultant bingeing destroy both your body and disables freedom in your life.

To get relief from the misery of a diet image and the eating disorders, you'll have to surrender to those fears. As it relates to thin(ner) supremacy body images, you would have to accept each of the following:

- *You will never be thinner.*

  - This requires you give up the shelter, narcissistic pride, aspirations, fantasies, and dreams of life in a thinner body.

  - All the times you allowed yourself to binge eat only because you assumed the weight gain would eventually get fixed, will never get fixed.

  - Clothes you purchased when you were thinner will need to be sifted through, boxed up, sold, or given away.

  - This might also mean you have to give up what you thought being thinner would give you: the spotlight, potential marital relationships or security, children, travel, easier mobility, and the idea you'd be healthier if you could be thinner.

  - By giving this up, you are essentially giving up any reason to diet now or in the future.

- *In order to accept that you'll never be thinner, you'll have to accept your current weight and all of its vulnerabilities, discomforts, and faults.*

  - This means you'll have to accept what has happened to your body as a result of bingeing, even though you wouldn't have binged if you knew the weight gain would never get fixed.

  - To accept your current body, you'd have to take responsibility for how your relationship with food has impacted your body, and that the physical discomfort you might be living with as a consequence of your dysfunctional relationship with food, *will never get fixed.*

  - You'll have to accept your fears of being stigmatized, seen as a failure, worthless to society, and you might end up being alone.

  - By accepting your current size and weight, you are essentially giving up any reason to diet now or in the future.

- *You must accept that the true nature of your body without dieting might be bigger than you are.*

  - For people who are anorexic and/or bulimic, it is inevitable that you must accept the truth of the genetics handed down to you from you parents, your grandparents, and thousands of years of generations before you.

  - For people who emotionally eat, without a diet you'll have to accept the inevitable weight gain as the consequence. Without disordered dieting and eating, you'll have to face the truth of your natural body, and that truth is probably bigger than the body you want.

✓ If the body you want demands obsessive/compulsive starvation, exercise, and purging to attain, it's a sure guarantee you'll gain weight by letting go of these disordered behaviors.

✓ If you hold onto dysfunctional eating as an emotional crutch, it is guaranteed your body will have to gain fat to sustain your life.

✓ Accepting that you'll gain weight means you'll have to buy comfortable clothes that fit, and that by accepting the risks and fact that you will gain weight, you are essentially giving up any reason to diet now or in the future.

· *If you lose weight without thought or effort because bingeing stops, you must stay unattached, noncommittal to it, and refuse to use it as a symbol of personal worth.*

– The goal is indifference to weight loss so that you're here and not there about it.

– It's the body's business if it naturally loses body fat, and if you attach to it, get too excited, inflate yourself with pride, or take credit for it as narcissistic supply, all of the disordered eating and fixation on your weight, pressure to diet, and the desire to eat excessively will return.

– By not caring about fat loss, you are essentially giving up on any reason to diet now or in the future.

- *If your body loses weight, you must accept that it will regain that lost weight.*

  - This means any lost weight you've attached pride and success to, might be regained if you give up the methods used for that weight loss.

  - If you can accept that at any time your body could lose and regain weight because its allowed to regulate itself, you are essentially giving up any reason to diet now or in the future.

It's easy to feel sorry for yourself for having to let go of the body image that seems to hold the keys to securing your third hierarchy of needs. Having a "poor-me" pity party, as if you're a martyr for having to let the body image go, is a last-ditch effort to keep the narcissistic supply of the eating disorder behaviors, even though they are incredibly abusive and harmful to your life.

Part of the problem is that it seems as if the fear, negative judgments, and feelings of victimhood and ruin about negative body image will be *permanent*, as if the feelings of emptiness and loss will be unrelenting for the rest of your life. Whereas dieting provides some sense of hope or possibility for achieving the body image of happiness—despite the fact it is only a fantasy or mirage. It seems as if you have only two choices, 1) vulnerability, fear, and assumed pain or 2) a hopeful fantasy and predictable misery.

On one hand, you could endure a tortured existence of abusing yourself with the diet image so you don't have to face the horror of losing the underlying body image. Or on the other hand, you could refuse to respond to that fear, and face excruciating terror and loss of the body image that feels like it will kill you. For this reason, it seems as if your enslavement to abusive diet-image behaviors are inescapable as you're held captive by your fears of life without the body image.

> **Most people feel safer in their disorder than they do the exposure of freedom from it. They'd rather stay inside the predictability of their suffering than to go into the vulnerability of the dangerous unknown.**

As exposure and vulnerability arises, before taking a moment to look at it, you're either binge eating as a feast before the next famine, obsessing over your next diet, exercising in the middle of the night, or seeking a bathroom or trashcan you can puke food into.

What family members and friends see are her weird, obsessive-compulsive behaviors, but what they don't see is the equally large fear and terror that those behaviors hide. Subsequently, when friends and family step in to help and try to block the self-harming behaviors, to the person suffering, in her mind their "help" is actually threatening her survival and adding to her terror. People who want to help end up being the enemy.

This is what happens for many people who've experienced a loved one struggling to leave an abusive relationship, or who has some form of trauma bonding, or Stockholm Syndrome. Threatening the abuser, in effect, feels to the victim as if you're threatening her survival.

When Family and Friends are the Enemy to Your Body-Diet Superior Syndrome

As family and friends open up about their fears and dislikes of the abusive eating and dieting behaviors, instead of responding with an open mind, the person suffering will typically react by being offended or even angry, especially if family contact and involvement causes more tension and strain within the controls of her disorder.

When a friend or family member who is encouraging recovery is in the way, or wants their loved one to end obsessive compulsive or "addictive" behaviors—to the person who is suffering, this feels like that helping person is actually harming you.

It seems as though the helping person is imprisoning, punishing, or making you live in terrorizing pain. It's like the person who wants you to stop the abuse really wants to be more important than your own survival. Those who are promoting recovery become a block or threat to your safety mechanisms, and this makes it seem as if they are the enemy.

> **MY EXPERIENCE:** *I remember feeling this way when being invited to eat in public, or when my family tried to step between me and my need to binge or purge.*
>
> *When a couple of my older sisters made personal and family sacrifices to help me when I was suffering with an eating disorder, they took time away from their family, financially supported me, and allowed me to live in their home, hoping to help me recover. Despite the love and care they gave me, I increased my efforts to hide and maintain the eating disorder behaviors that I desperately needed to quit. So that they wouldn't know I was still relying on these behaviors, I'd secretly puke food up in a wastebasket in my room, and flush it down the toilet when I'd go to the bathroom. I'd exercise quietly, go for runs in the middle of the night, and I'd even work excessively around the house and yard as a way to "help" them clean and take care of their home. However, my true intention in helping was to burn calories in order to stay thin.*
>
> *All of my thoughts and actions were positioned to secretly defend my eating disorder behavior, even when others were sacrificing and giving of themselves to help me recover. The truth is, as much as I did want relief, I didn't know how to surrender my survival needs,*

even when those needs hurt other people. And as loved ones stepped in, my issues became worse as my defense of the behaviors intensified. As I clutched harder to those impulses, the more determined others were to try to take them from me.

I'd pretend like I was "all better," and use language I knew would convince them I was healthy—but I knew underneath it all that I wanted and needed my destructive behaviors.

The results were:

- *I wasn't going to let anybody stop me, even if it was my parents.*

- *If, for whatever reason, I didn't have access to my eating disorder behavior, I would experience intense rage and anger, and would act out in a destructive way.*

- *I knew my anger was wrong.*

- *I knew what I was doing was bizarre, but anger served as a way to get and do what I needed in order to rid myself from feelings of terror.*

- *I didn't know how to stop, and I felt like a psychotic caged animal fighting to survive.*

The rage I experienced wasn't against them, as much as it was a frantic fight for what I believed my life needed in order to survive. I knew I was out of my mind, but the terror of not having any self-defense against what felt was like a torturous death, seemed far worse than the judgment and hurt I caused other people.

It's not that I didn't desperately want to please and succeed for my family, but they were blocking me from my protective eating disorder behavior. In my mind, this made it seem as if they were adding to and reinforcing threats to my survival.

Imagine you are a family member to a person suffering from what I described. If you get in the way of what she needs, you get attacked, even if you're a caretaker or loved one. You accommodate, take care of her needs, provide safety, comfort, and support, yet when she feels threatened, your efforts and sacrifices are taken for granted, and you might even get blamed for her suffering.

When a person in eating disorder pain seeks my help, I'm not surprised when her anger turns toward me as she believes that I'm withholding her survival needs, and that by suggesting she let go and escape, I am also reinforcing the source of her misery. She thinks my recommendations are blocking her from her desperately needed coping mechanisms, making her a martyr because she's can't be safe in the miserable behavior she's seeking to remove from her life. Being a victim of having to let it all go eventually cycles a person back to the same abusive patterns, and the same suffering over and over again. Being a slave to these behaviors eventually becomes hopelessly miserable without reward, *and the only way to escape is to voluntarily and intentionally give it up.*

Voluntarily giving up the diet image means giving up the body image, and ultimately this has to be a personal decision that isn't about pleasing anyone or wanting anyone's approval. *It's about freedom.*

MY EXPERIENCE: *For me, it wasn't until I was suffering badly enough, and was in such intense psychological distress that I was internally willing to voluntarily give up my behaviors. To do this I had to be willing to face the threats, horror, and anguish those be-*

haviors hid without going into martyrdom—and it wasn't until then that true recovery opened up to me.

It was a decision I had to make, no matter what anybody else thought about it. I couldn't afford to surrender my survival to face apparent death, with the pressure of gratifying someone else's needs—not even my parents or husband. It had to be 100 percent for and by myself. Up until that point, no amount of education, love from family, consequences, or destruction was worth it. There was no amount of pleading or family pain that would keep me from my destructive survival needs. I was slowly killing myself…while trying to survive.

When the culture you live in, or maybe it's your own spouse, family, and friends, approach a singular body image with strict, unwavering, totalitarian reinforcement, and they shame and criticize anyone who's body doesn't match—releasing yourself from having to achieve that image would require that you accept their judgment, ridicule, and rejection without feeling ashamed or that you deserve to be abandoned. Otherwise, you'll continue to protect yourself in hope that the worst-case scenario you fear, doesn't happen. This is a continuation of the syndrome—and ultimately you won't escape the diet images and body images holding you captive inside the psychological containment that harms you.

And until you surrender the martyr role and the victim position, you will continue to defend, rationalize, and argue for the benefits of the disorder that keep you coming back despite the isolation, darkness, abuse, and misery that you want to escape.

When Loss is Freedom

One of the hardest things to see when you are suffering inside an eating disorder is why something so damaging and miserable *could feel so vital and important to keeping you alive.*

But at the same time, you'd do anything to relieve yourself from it. In my case, because my standards of fitness and leanness weren't negotiable, the only way I could imagine relief from the work, isolation, and perfectionism they demanded was to commit suicide. It wasn't until I looked at the option of permanently losing my body's thinness, "health," and fitness that a clear and obvious end to the eating disorder presented itself.

However, letting go of these standards meant that I'd have to face the ugly truth these ideals covered up. As much as I was desperate for relief, I wasn't necessarily desperate enough to surrender my safety. *In my mind, to stop dieting, bingeing, purging, controlling food, and impulsively exercising would be like accepting a traumatic death. It wasn't until I was literally facing death that I made this connection.*

- I could see that if I was unwilling to let go of these behaviors that suicide was the only escape.

- If I was voluntarily willing to let my eating-disorder behaviors go, there might be hope for a new life and a true and permanent recovery.

- This would entail I permanently accept that my body would no longer be "superior," and that other people would know I was a fraud, and a failure.

- It was at this point that I realized my pride and fear of criticism was the real reason I wasn't willing to let go of my diet, exercise, and body images.

- *I held myself hostage to behaviors that damaged my life all because I was unwilling to face real or perceived judgment and disapproval.*

Up until that moment I believed my eating disorder was "safe," and was something I justified and needed. I rationalized and reasoned for why it was important, despite the fact that I was considering suicide to relieve myself from its misery and pursuant hell.

But when that safety requires isolation and a life filled with complete and total misery, there comes a point when the pain and anguish you've been avoiding is no different or might even be better than the misery and suffering you've been surviving with.

It is at this moment that people I work with are willing to let go of their miserable "safety" to face the dangerous pain that their eating disorder protects them from.

Like a person held captive who reaches the point where she'd rather die than to continue, there's no risk in facing the potential death that might occur when attempting to escape. Either way, there's loss, but at least by escaping there is hope for freedom—even if you don't know what that freedom is. It's more hopeful to face the risk of death as you escape, than to accept certain torture and eventual death by suicide.

At this point, threats that previously had held you hostage from trying to escape now have no power. There's no amount of fear-based coercion and threats of loss that is worth suffering for, because you'd rather die. And in relation to suffering to death—being ugly, alone, or physically limited seem relatively easy, especially if that's all it takes to gain freedom.

- *"No one will love you!"*

  - You'd rather be free and alone than fake, miserable, and accepted.

- *"Everyone will find out you're a failure, and that you couldn't handle it!"*

  - You'd rather face the embarrassment of being seen and exposed as a failure, and accept disapproval and rejection without defense. Embarrassment is a fleeting emotion compared to suffering permanently while trying to prove otherwise in fear of other people's opinion.

- *"You're going to live in pain and unhealth if you don't lose weight."*

  - You'd rather have sore knees and Type 2 diabetes than to continue to suffer with perpetual anxiety, fear, and shame about food as you binge before and after the next diet.

When death seems relieving to a person who has suffered so intensely while fighting for something, and she is humble enough to admit failure, the only other option is to let go of the fantasy she's been chasing, and then quit that miserable life, doing so in exchange for the unknown.

What before seemed too scary and impossible to accept, is now a direct path to freedom, even if that means living in a body that is limiting, stigmatized, and a source of criticism.

MY EXPERIENCE: *I remember the moment I humbly surrendered to the failure. Instead of feeling sorry for myself, a sadness and grief washed over me. I had to look at the loss and hurt that my efforts to "win" had cost my life. It was tragic to me—the level of suffering I had willfully accepted and clutched onto, despite the darkness and death it brought to my life. Yes, I had fallen in "love" with the eating disorder to the point where I almost committed suicide over the suffering that came with it—because I had refused to give it up.*

Dieting and extreme exercise, and obsessive body measuring were my protective rescuers, and bingeing brought fun and excitement to a life of hunger, loneliness, and isolation. Despite the horrendous demands these relationships required, I bonded to them as if my life depended on it. However, as these behaviors became a larger and larger comfort, my life had to fit into a smaller and smaller cage, and to escape I had to willfully let go of these relationships, even though under the circumstance, they were important coping mechanisms that provided comfort, protection, and a shield from what I thought I couldn't handle.

Bingeing felt euphoric only because I desperately needed freedom from the authoritarian dieting, fear of food, and shame for eating. Exercise and purging wouldn't have been so impulsive if I didn't have such intense fear and shame about the feelings of getting fatter. Like people divorcing, I had to accept failure, and grieve the loss of those relationships and what they gave me, under the circumstance. But as I was quitting and escaping that circumstance, I had to say goodbye to that life and those behaviors for good, and this was truly sad.

However, as I grieved the losses, I knew that if given a second chance, I wouldn't...

- Choose to binge,

- Want to obsess about food,

- Choose to relate to exercise in such an abusive manner,

- Care about my weight and size, and

- Choose to follow diets with moral vigilance.

This is the case with all of the people I've worked with. I've never heard a person who suffers from binge eating disorder say that she actually wants to binge. I've never met a bulimic who delights in making herself puke—or an emaciated anorexic who enjoys starving herself. These are the behaviors they desperately want recovery from, but the only way to get that recovery is to 1) admit that way of life has been a total failure and 2) accept the permanent loss of what they emotionally get out of those behaviors.

Like a battered wife secretly escaping and leaving behind everything she thought was shelter and safety, or the enslaved captive sneaking out in the middle of the night—*escaping an eating disorder and the syndrome that keeps you clutching to it, requires accepting the truth of your body and the truth of your life without using diets and excessive eating to cope.* You are surrendering a life you know so well in order to start a new life you know nothing about.

Ultimately, you'll need to relearn who you are, how you want to relate to food, and what you want in life. You will need to recover.

"If you want to awaken all of humanity, then awaken all of yourself. If you want to eliminate the suffering in the world, then eliminate all that is dark and negative in yourself. Truly the greatest gift you have to give is that of your own self-transformation."

– Lao Tzu

Chapter 11

Leaving Safety and Control
for the Vulnerability of Freedom

"Truth is a force of transformation, which is why people fear the truth. Truth always causes change. There is no such thing as absorbing the power of a truth and having your life remain the same."

— Caroline Myss, author and spiritual healer

Email from YouTube follower in her 30's:

Hi Robin, I've been following your YouTube videos for a while and feel as if you're someone I can really talk to. I've reached a point in my life where I'm at my wits end. I have battled my weight since I was a teenager. I've never really been skinny and for a long time, I was okay with it. Like you said, those were the years I didn't have issues with food. About a year ago I decided to do the ketogenic diet, with intermittent fasting, and lost about 35 pounds. Since then, I've lost and then regained 20 of those pounds this year too. The reason for this is because I will follow the diet for about a month or two, and then I end up gaining anywhere from 10–15 pounds back because I go on bingeing/purging or just bingeing sprees. So, I eventually get back on the wagon and diet strictly to re-lose the weight. I am getting so obsessive over my weight and so emotionally drained from all the dieting that I have now developed an anxiety disorder and have had frequent panic attacks over it.

I feel that I am ALWAYS on a diet and cannot enjoy my life for fear of gaining the weight back. I have avoided social situations where I know there will be food and/or drinking present so instead of enjoying my life, I shut myself in. Other times when I allow myself to indulge, I completely go on an all-out bingeing spree, and I feel horrible about myself shortly after. I used to binge and purge, but now I've gotten past the purging and just end up bingeing and living with the discomfort after. Sometimes I feel as if dieting has been the best and worst thing that ever happened to me. At first it allowed me to lose weight and lose weight quickly. However, if I add back in the "normal" foods, it causes me to gain weight so easily that it frustrates me, and then I give up and go back to old eating habits (bingeing, or just unhealthy eating). I get depressed about the weight I have put back on, and I can't help but to go back to dieting. As I mentioned before, this means that I avoid going out, which really drains and frustrates me.

Currently I am strictly dieting and losing the weight. I really, really, really, do not want to go into that "dark place" again by bingeing and gaining the weight back and definitely DO NOT want to diet this way anymore. I realize it isn't realistic. But for now, I need to lose the weight. I would really love to have my sanity back again and stop worrying and being so obsessive about gaining weight. I just want to lose weight and be free from thinking about it.

I realize that I have been rambling and I apologize for that, but I feel that you, being experienced with dieting, bingeing, and eating disorders would have more understanding of these kinds of things. Watching your YouTube videos, I often thought to myself, "If only I lived in her area, I would love to have her to talk to. You really seem to "get it."

I realize you must be very busy but I would greatly appreciate any words of advice or even if you have a colleague in your field that you may know or recommend that lives in the Southern California area that I may consult with, preferably with your similar expertise (fat chance I know, but it's worth asking). Any words are greatly and tremendously appreciated.

Escaping Body Image and Facing Death— When Suicide Seems Like the ONLY Choice

Imagine you live in a dark space or box that relieves you from living in perpetual anxiety, fear, and terror, but life inside the safety of that box feels very small, dark, cold, and isolating. Inside that small space, all you have in your mind are thoughts about the right and wrong food, diets, body fat, exercise, how much fat you have, how much you weigh, what your body measurements are, what food you can eat, and constant shame and panic for eating food you aren't supposed to eat. Your entire life is confined inside that dark box, a slave to single-minded fixation seeking relief from the terror and fears you have about food and your body, while others around you live in the sunshine—open and uninhibited to think and be how they want.

This is how distraught I felt when I had an eating disorder, and why I felt I had no other choice but to commit suicide. From inside that box, it seemed as if there was no way out and no possibility that my mind would be released from my need for the fanatical levels of thinking, focus, work, organization, and complete emotional and physical engrossment on maintaining the safety of my eating disorder.

For years, I didn't know how to describe an eating disorder other than to describe living in misery in that dark box, and to say it's a severe mental illness that destroys your life and body.

A more difficult question to answer:

How did I go from having severe mental illness that resulted in the relieving choice to kill myself, to being completely and permanently liberated from it?

I wondered: With an "addiction" or a genetic disease or disorder, is it possible to so quickly be pardoned from that illness, and then feel permanently freed?

For me, being set free was like a miracle. However, that miracle was a matter of cognitive choices that I made and, in the end, had total power over. Although it didn't seem that way, ultimately I had to completely abandon my beliefs, and I had to be willing to expose myself to face what felt like complete and total terror and death, in order to get that freedom. Without both, I know for a fact that I'd be dead. For my full story (*My Weight-Loss Apocalypse*), is downloadable on my website: http://WeightLossApocalyse.com

For a long time, I didn't know how to describe how I went from being enslaved in terror and darkness inside that box, to being liberated into a space of love, grace, and peace. Today, I commonly use the word "recover" to describe this shift because it's a simple description that resonates with most people. But for me, "recovery" is not the right word.

> **A more accurate way to describe going from the torment inside that dark space, to then be permanently unshackled from it, would be that I escaped. Recovery was a process I experienced *after* I escaped.**

When looking into mental illness (like an eating disorder), it is described as an "addiction" or a predisposed genetic problem that's likely passed down family lineage. Mental illness can often be relieved with medication, and can be managed with therapy, but it isn't something people simply stop having. When eating disorders are described this way, and are explained as an addiction or disease that must be managed, this makes me wonder why I haven't suffered or felt impelled to go back into that dark box since the day I left it. If the eating disorder I experienced was an addiction, today I'd still be managing desires to binge, anxiety about body fat, and impulses to puke and exercise after I ate "dangerous" food.

The extreme levels of fear and terror I experienced was not a choice, and it wasn't "imagined." The fight-or-flight response I had wasn't a choice either. However, where I think my escape happened was in the choice to do the opposite of what my mind was telling me to do. I chose to be unresponsive to my genetics and tens of thousands of years of evolutionary wiring that demanded I run and hide with bingeing, and to fight and protect myself with dieting, puking, and exercise. I willfully and intentionally surrendered my life to what I believed would destroy my existence and who I was. However, I am certain this willingness had a lot to do with the fact that I had decided to kill myself. I had nothing to lose by surrendering my eating disorder, and facing complete and total destruction.

While preparing to die, and humbly contemplating where things went wrong, I realized my narcissistic fear of fat gain was actually a terrorizing fear of death that felt more like murder.

Fear and angst that impel people to avoid danger is prewired through hundreds of thousands of years of evolution that is geared to protect, defend, and preserve life. This default reaction to perceived vulnerability isn't a choice, and it certainly isn't a disorder. But when it's connected to beliefs that don't align with reality, that's where the "disorder" and problem exists. Unfortunately, resultant struggle and suffering that's blamed on faults of the believer rather than the unrealistic belief, is how abusive cultural dogma, like foot binding or thin(ner) supremacy, is perpetuated. Eventually, courageous believers will have to admit failure and accept criticism and judgment *in order to quit and free themselves from a lifetime of dedication to goals that aren't achievable.*

The truth is, no goal should require people to sacrifice years and decades of freedom in their life. Nobody should have to live in misery, performing for someone else's approval. Ultimately, people have to "fail" the goal and quit in order to free themselves from being dedicated to it, and from feeling bad about themselves for letting it go. This clarity is what I hope each and every person I work with *can see for herself.*

Ask yourself:

- ✓ If the goal is unrealistic and unachievable without you feeling isolated, obsessive and dedicated for the rest of your life, is it worth it?

✓ Should you feel bad about yourself for not succeeding at it?

✓ Is it something to be ashamed of—if you fail at a goal that requires mental illness to achieve?

Without accepting others' disapproval ahead of time, it would be natural and so much easier for her to go back into hiding, and to pick up her goals and eating disorder behaviors instead. But when those mechanisms are what's destroying her life, to be set free from them, she'll have to face the terror she's been avoiding, without defense. However…*facing fear and what seems to threaten your life is not how we are wired.*

To escape, a person will have to do the opposite of what his or her genetic predisposition demands.

We aren't wired to accept rejection and abandonment or that we might end up alone. But when a person willfully surrenders and refuses abusive measures like narcissistic body and diet images, it's unavoidable that the horror of being exposed as inferior will wash over her.

MY EXPERIENCE: *I know for me, it seemed easier to binge, purge, over-exercise, measure, and obsess over food and my body every day, all day long, than was experiencing pain and terror of losing the safety of my body image. This was true until I came to the point where living that way made life feel mercilessly unbearable, and I couldn't imagine continuing to live another day.*

I'd look forward to going to sleep every night because that was the only period of time I experienced relief. I assumed it wasn't an option to face the fearful terror my eating disorder protected me from, so when my eating and exercise behavior became so unrelentingly miserable, and the suffering from it was mercilessly toxic, the only way I could imagine relief was to kill myself.

Suicide felt light, forgiving, and free, and once I finally decided that it was going to happen, I felt incredibly liberated. However, as I emotionally prepared and contemplated the terror of death that I'd inevitably experience moments before committing suicide, I realized this terror was the exact same terror that my eating disorder helped me avoid and hide from.

This is when I saw clearly that I had lost this battle—and I had some choices to make.

It was unavoidable that I would have to face the terror, whether moments before slitting my wrists or pulling the trigger of a gun pointed at my head, or as I surrendered my eating disorder weapons and defense mechanisms to hold up a white flag in defeat. Like a lost battle in war, I could either avoid admitting the loss by killing myself, or I could face the terror of surrendering to the truth and accept the loss of the body image, in humility.

I could see that what it would take to commit suicide was exactly what it would take to face the terror of losing the body image that my eating disorder behaviors served and protected.

If I willfully let go of my eating disorder, and surrendered the body image those behaviors served, I'd have to face the terror of exposure and the emptiness that I felt inside. Once facing that terror and accepting the inevitable result, the body and diet image I held myself captive to would lose importance and power. If I survived, the original person I was born to be might have hope for freedom and a new life.

The truth is, my way of surviving was a complete and total failure, and for the first time I was humble enough to admit it. This was my personal war and my personal loss, even though I dedicated every ounce of my identity, purpose, and life to the belief systems of a thinner, fitter, healthier, and sexier body image. I was thin enough, fit enough, and attractive enough, but what it took to achieve this destroyed my soul and any hope for joy, happiness, and freedom in life.

For the first time, it didn't make sense to feel sorry for myself, have a pity party, or to in any way position myself as a martyr for having to let it all go. I had to admit to myself: this was a failure of my own doing. And if I could accept and admit that loss, and was liberated from the insanity and darkness I experienced in my mind, I was NOT a victim…it would be a miracle.

I realized that if the level of forcefulness and dedication I gave toward reaching the mirage of body image wasn't good enough—that maybe I didn't really want to "win." I'd rather quit and admit I couldn't handle it, even if it meant I'd live forever as a reject, a loser, and stigmatized as a worthless failure. At least with that admittance, even though I might be alone, there was hope for my soul to be liberated in that freedom.

When a person suffering this way admits failure to the belief system she's been holding herself hostage to—and is willing to expose that inadequacy and loss to the world, all the while accepting ridicule, disapproval, and the inevitable truth of other's response—the door to escape opens and freedom presents itself.

Every single person I've worked with believed her eating disorder behavior would bring her that freedom. This is what people think they'll achieve when they pursue achieving body and diet images. They are wanting to transcend the lower survival hierarchies of need, and also reach higher levels of consciousness, where they can experience the expansion of the mind through curiosity and exploration. Unfortunately, when depending on body images to validate your worth and value, that threaten your access to food, this freedom doesn't exist, except as a fantasy or mirage.

The second point, or condition I listed as part of the Body-Diet Supremacy Syndrome is that the persons suffering has:

> 2. *A personal position of needing external validation from others to secure his or her third hierarchy of need—to feel worthy of love, inclusion, and acceptance.*

Ultimately, when a person is willing to surrender the diet and body images used to supply this validation, she is positioning herself to internally secure her own needs. As she exposes 1) the truth of her body, and 2) the truth of her inadequacy to comply, and 3) accepts the vulnerable truth of other's response—*without needing to hide or defend herself*—she is acting in courage and changing the vulnerability and source of security to her third hierarchy of need.

Securing Your Third Hierarchy of Need

Maslow's third hierarchy of need *to feel lovable and belong* is far more complicated and complex than the first and second more important and stronger needs that are required for life. The third hierarchy of need isn't essential to stay alive like food is, but it has evolved as a need that has great impact on our emotional wellbeing. Access to food and shelter is straightforward, whereas relationships with others is vulnerable to 1) your ability to take care of yourself, 2) how you feel about yourself, and 3) how others feel about you.

Securing this hierarchy of need relies heavily on our own perception of personal worth, as well as our sense of capacity to survive if we are left on our own.

If you could independently adapt to challenge and find a way to provide your own needs, chances are you'd be less impacted by negative criticism than someone who is highly dependent on others to survive. And when you experience judgment and criticism, with a personal sense of worth, you're less likely to be triggered into self-defense, *or take it personally.*

A sense of personal capacity to adapt and learn skills necessary to take care of oneself is described as *competence.* Competence is what drives the energy and aptitude necessary to teach oneself, or to figure out how to make it on your own. Without competence, a person's need for other's approval goes up, and his or her need to "fit in" and receive validation would increase.

> **When dependent on others, feeling unwanted, unneeded, unappreciated, without value, lonely, or without something to give, would justifiably elicit emotional triggers of life-or-death stress.**

Without personally securing oneself first, symptoms of survival mode, such as anxiety, competition, paranoia, perfectionism, and the pressure to perform, would drive much of the mental state and work of an individual. But, as these survival emotions might increase productivity and willingness to conform, they also might increase emotional tension between one's mind and the need for external validation.

You will ultimately function in the lower more primitive survival states of consciousness, which are victim-oriented, defensive, and focused inward towards egocentric self-preservation, fear, and loss.

For someone in the lower states of consciousness, like apathy, facing fear and discussing her shame is a big deal. Facing underlying issues can be extremely frightening—and very difficult to accept. But if you can have the courage to come out of hiding and are willing to face the vulnerability of the issues, you will experience a rise in consciousness to have both hope and energy to live.

Every aspect of suffering in states of survival mode plays an important part of human evolution. It's easy to judge these aspects of ourselves because they are truthfully miserable.

- However, without the misery of these mechanisms, what would inspire us to learn and evolve outside the discomforts of these self-centered limitations?

- What would motivate us to transcend primitive defense mechanisms into a higher more open state of consciousness?

I know for me, if it weren't for such horror and misery in my own suffering, I wouldn't have opened myself up to suicide, and from there I wouldn't have questioned why my life hit such a low level of existence. It took complete and utter failure for me to surrender my pride, to accept failure, and to open myself to the truth.

The incredible thing is that every aspect of growth is a steppingstone, with the ultimate goal being to secure our primitive survival needs, and to transcend narcissistic self-preservation into the open life of experience, exploration, and enlightenment. However, until our basic human needs are met, these higher levels of existence won't be available.

You will come out of survival mode and in a relatively higher level of consciousness if:

- Your relationship with food is relatively safe. You feel secure that you have enough, can share, and can get more. You aren't afraid of food and don't restrict in fear. Food is enjoyable, eating is functional, and without need to clutch onto it or overindulge.

- Your perception of the environment is adaptable, and you feel secure in your ability to handle challenge. You could live in a bigger or smaller home, have a nicer car or not. Your need for things is not here nor there. Things are nice, but nothing is necessary. If someone else needed your clothes, you'd give them away.

- Your sense of lovability and belonging is fulfilled from within and is generally unconditional and gracious towards oneself and others. Even if you aren't accepted, are rejected, and people don't like you, there is a sense of worth that comes from life within. Mistakes are a normal and healthy aspect of life. Relationships are functional, forgiving, and aren't demanding.

- You accept death and are not afraid to take calculated risks in life. There is open potential in life to be experienced, explored, and enjoyed.

In order to fulfill Maslow's *third hierarchy of need to belong*, it's not a matter of getting rid of the primitive sensitivity to being rejected and abandoned, but rather bypassing it with self-competence, using courage and grace to be real with oneself and others. You are essentially developing a sense of strength and capacity to be judged, ridiculed, and rejected, without defining yourself as unworthy of love and inclusion. This is true even when it's inevitable that others might not like or approve of you *if you don't conform to their needs.* It's not that you shouldn't "fit in," and adapt to your environment, but that you don't define yours or other's worth based on that ability.

Revealing the truth without blame, fault, excuse or defense is an act of courage that frees you up from having to prove something different. You are free to be who you truthfully are, and are given grace from believing things that are intended to force you to be something you aren't.

When the terror of being different or unworthy is exposed, and the vulnerability of others' response is intentionally faced, felt, and accepted, the truth of reality is set free to reveal itself.

In the case of survival that's attached to body and diet images, to rise above the lower-most important survival hierarchies of need, and to elevate the level of awareness beyond self-preservation, you'd have to display the courage necessary to admit you've failed the beliefs and standards of the narcissistic body and diet images, and accept exclusion from the people and cultures who won't otherwise accept you.

Grieving the Loss, Exposing the Truth, and Accepting Reality

When people realize and clearly see they will never recover from the torment, isolation, darkness, and terror of insecure survival mechanisms unless they admit failure, surrender their defense mechanisms, and face the loss of the idealistic goals, they are presented with a choice.

- You could keep the known benefits of the body image, dieting, and emotional eating, but you are consciously choosing to suffer.

- Or you could willfully surrender the benefits, and you'll be set free from both. You are no longer held to those goals and the means to achieving those goals.

When admitting failure and letting body and diet images go, most people describe incredible sadness. This sadness is very different from what they experienced previously, which was self-pity, anger, and victimhood. It feels more like the somber grief you'd expect after the loss of war, or a permanent death.

This is like realizing and admitting your marriage has failed, and that divorce is necessary. You must let go and grieve "as it's gone," the good times and the fantasy of what you thought the relationship could be. And despite the immense freedom and relief that comes from ending a tortured existence, there is loss, and with grief, eventually comes *acceptance.* Acceptance means you fully grasp the loss and have humbly surrendered to every aspect of it.

Being set free from narcissistic body and diet images would open you up to vulnerability and exposure as you're presented with a new existence that is limitless and has immense freedom and independence from having to be and do what others demand. This is like escaping a totalitarian religious cult, *even though you have no concept of who you are or how to function outside of it.*

This means you are leaving everything you know behind, to enter a new life you know nothing about, but with the competence to know you have the integrity to handle and accept the truth of life as it reveals itself.

As you escape survival mechanisms that hold you hostage to appease others' narcissistic demands, you are freed to recover the truth of yourself and the life you want to live. This escape into recovery is like a do-over—as if you're given the room to learn and grow like a child. You're allowed the grace and forgiveness to figure things out, to explore, and learn without fear of being disgraced or disapproved of. Except this time, you are responsible to that grace to be truthful about your humanness, and to participate in the life you want, while fitting in with others and your society without taking yourself so seriously. You are set free and liberated to direct the life you want.

Email from YouTube follower in her 40's:

Robin, I'm writing this to thank you. I've had, through your book and videos, been learning so much. This morning I had this light-bulb moment where I was like... My body is awesome! I was looking at it and thinking, holy cow! I am 200 pounds and never thought it was possible to accept myself and the way I look at this weight until now.

Without the shame and fear about my body, I do NOT ever have to diet, binge, or purge again! Ever! I will never feel bad about food again! My body will heal, more slowly, but it will! My health is good on its own. Eat to hunger, no guilt, NO diets, be accountable. HOW FREEING is that! I'm overwhelmed and feeling euphoric, I know I will have to keep reminding myself if these things, but it's AMAZING! For a while now I've been trying to do what you said, which was to unapologetically sit in my self-pity, pain, anxiety, boredom, and depression. I've been hating it and feeling sorry for myself. But it dawned on me this morning that if I don't have to fight and hide from insecurity anymore, then my life would be set free to just be. This too shall pass, so enjoy it! This was so relieving. And because of this, I get to sit in this euphoria! Feel it, be present, enjoy it! When we sit in our crap, we don't have to suffer trying to avoid it! There is so much freedom and joy knowing I can handle it! I don't know if I'm making sense, but I have to thank you with my heart, soul and awesome body! Thank you! You're truly so talented and amazing. Thank you for sharing you, so I can find me!

"One day, I had to sit down with myself and decide that I loved myself, no matter what my body looked like and what other people thought about my body."

– Gabourey Sibide, Actress

Chapter 12

Hope, Hope, and More Hope

"You will learn a lot from yourself if you stretch in the direction of goodness, of bigness, of kindness, of forgiveness, of emotional bravery. Be a warrior for love."

– Cheryl Strayed, author

In Search of the Truth…
Question the Way You Think and What You're Afraid of.

Most of what I do with people when they seek my help is to give them perspective. I'm doing nothing other than giving them a different vantage point to look at why they're doing what they're doing, so they can understand what they'll need to give up and let go of in order to be free from the behaviors they want recovery from.

> **Besides discussing theories on survival mode, Maslow's hierarchy of needs, evolutionary psychology, narcissistic cultural dogma, body image, and thin supremacy…I spend a great deal of time asking clients clarifying questions.**

I know for me, when I believed the misery of my eating-disorder behaviors were inescapable, and subsequently I decided to end my life—as I prepared for suicide, there were questions that came to my mind. These questions specifically uncovered why I was clutching to the behaviors that defined the eating disorder. I sought to answer those exposing questions truthfully—even if the truth uncomfortably challenged my beliefs and my identity. My answers came from a place of humility, seeking understanding rather than a way to defend myself or justify the disordered survival behaviors I was killing myself with. Today, I try to do the same when I ask questions of the person who is seeking the same clarity.

However, at first some people give me answers that are based on impulse, based on their fears, and based on protecting and reaffirming their brainwashed body-image dogma. In those cases, I refuse their answer, because they aren't telling the heartfelt truth, nor will they escape if they continue to defend the abuse. Sometimes I have to ask the same question 2–5 times before a person actually thinks deeper, allows for their discomfort, and gives a truthful answer. When she gets past the mentally constructed answer to seek the truth from her heart and soul, she experiences what it feels like to be humble, to be vulnerable, and to be released from defending narcissistic aspects of the dogma. *The truth does set you free.*

There is freedom and peace in facing the vulnerable truth to humbly admit complete and total failure, without blame, self-defense, or excuse. It means you are liberated from having to fight to prove otherwise, and permanently free from having to defend yourself from that threat.

If you are wanting freedom from beliefs that shame you, behaviors that hurt you, and dogma that controls you, *ask yourself the questions you don't want to answer.* Be honest even if it hurts your fearful ego. Look at your life from a viewpoint that isn't comfortable. Have courage to tell the truth, to be alone if that's what the truth entails, and to take responsibility for navigating and directing the life you are living in a way that brings you joy. When you open yourself up to the truth, you are opening yourself up to forgive yourself, to forgive others, and to forgive the rigid rules that keep you confined. Living in grace with the truth gives you freedom and a life you will feel worthy of living.

Ask yourself and answer *truthfully:*

- ✓ How would your life change if all forms of dieting and weight loss were removed forever?

- ✓ What would change if you had to be 100 pounds heavier, for the rest of your life? No amount of exercise, dieting, or surgery could change it.

- ✓ If your true natural body is larger than the "ideal," would you willfully focus on dieting and restricting food for the rest of your life, to force your body to be thinner than it's supposed to be? Knowing that the focus on your weight would have to be permanent?

✓ What would happen to your eating disorder of you got in a car accident and permanently lost the use of your legs? If you lost your eyesight? Lost your hearing? Your entire face and body got burned in a fire and you are permanently disfigured and scarred? Etc., etc.

✓ If it meant *permanent* freedom from having to fixate on food, focus on restriction, being obsessed with your body, and ashamed and in fear of gaining weight, would you be willing to permanently agree to accept a larger body? Would you be willing to live the rest of your life and all of life's adventures in that larger body?

✓ What would happen to bingeing and emotional eating if there were no diets, no food judgments, no food guidelines, no "good" or "bad" foods, no "you should eat less" statements, and no concept of "health" attached to food?

✓ If you won the "food lottery" and was awarded freedom from all food criticisms and judgments and awarded all of the food you could imagine from all over the world, to eat at any time, in any quantity, for any reason, forever—would you continue to overeat or binge knowing the food will never go away? How would your relationship with food change?

✓ If God or your creator came to you and said:

> "You are free from ever having to care about your weight. *Fixing your body wasn't supposed to be your purpose in this life.* Whether you're fatter or thinner isn't what your life is supposed to be about! The more you focus on food, worry about your weight, and fixate on your size and

health, the less freedom you have to live your life and to experience your true purpose. No matter what your weight and size, you are to stop caring about your body and your "health," and you are to open your mind to live this life *right now*. Nothing about your body needs to be fixed. Forgive yourself and move on. You are free to create a life that can change and evolve in a way so that you can experience life to the fullest, and when its time for this life to end, you don't have to worry about that either."

What would you do? Would you willfully choose to continue to fixate on your body, your weight, food, and needing to diet? Or would you accept freedom and move on with your life?

✓ What would it feel like to accept that you've always done the best you could with what you thought was the right thing to do? Even when you clearly made mistakes or made decisions that you regret? No matter what has happened to your body, to your relationships with people, and to your life—what would it feel like to recognize it is all understandable and completely forgivable? That you and all of the people who might have hurt you are worthy of grace, forgiveness, and mercy?

In Conclusion

"Don't wait until everything is just right. It will never be perfect. There will always be challenges, obstacles and less than perfect conditions. So what. Get started now. With each step you take, you will grow stronger and stronger, more and more skilled, more and more self-confident and more and more successful."

– Mark Victor Hansen, author

Over the years, I've had the opportunity to observe full recovery from people who've suffered with eating disorders from all over the spectrum. I've also been able to witness continued struggles and frustration as people strain gripping onto their desires and wanting to be thinner and diet, as well as wanting to eat as an emotional coping mechanism. One of the greatest blocks in people's recovery is when they think freedom is an all-or-nothing process.

For some people, freedom comes to them permanently and abruptly. For others, it comes in waves because of the different stages of humility the process requires.

More often than not, escaping and recovery is a trial-and-error process of letting go—like a battered woman that leaves and then returns to her abuser over and over again. It takes *letting go to know freedom does exist, and for some people it takes a return to suffering to get clarity about the truth, and to accept what needs to be surrendered, faced, and accepted.* As people go back and forth between freedom and suffering, when they give themselves grace and wiggle room to figure it out, eventually they clearly see the lies of the fantasy, and they finally let it go completely. This is the point when their mind is free to explore life, and they've learned they don't need or want another captor that keeps them trapped in fear and self-defense.

What it takes for a person to eventually get complete and total freedom and then recovery is unique to her personal willingness to face her own mortality, and to accept that by giving herself grace to figure it all out, she can handle it.

With courage to stop defending oneself from threats of rejection and abandonment that trigger her third hierarchy of need, she is set free from that need that's defining and controlling her mind. With courage to face survival threats to her "health" and body that trigger her first and second hierarchies of need, she is released from being a servant to fix or hide from those fears. When fear of her own body and food loses its power, and the anxiety and pressure to micromanage food, diet, exercise, and concepts of "health" lose importance—the mind is set free to be more rational and balanced about caring for her body. By surrendering to the vulnerability of death, a person who previously was a slave to those survival mechanisms, is set free to determine for herself, what's worth fighting and suffering for and what isn't. This is the space of openness and freedom that exists after you escape, as well as the rebirth and recovery of your truth.

This quote from Haruki Murakami perfectly describes what I experienced once I escaped and then recovered. My hope is that you, too, can come out of the storm different than the person who walked into it.

> *"And once the storm is over, you won't remember how you made it through, how you managed to survive. You won't even be sure, whether the storm is really over. But one thing is certain. When you come out of the storm, you won't be the same person who walked in. That's what this storm's all about."*

– Japanese writer, Haruki Murakami

Messages of Hope

I've compiled messages from people who've worked through the process, either working with me directly or trying to figure it out on their own by following sessions I've posted on my YouTube channel. The goal with this chapter is to inspire hope that freedom is possible.

45-year-old Woman Suffering with Bulimia

Message: I watch your videos every day. I've had an eating disorder since I was 12…I'm 45 now. Listening to the struggles of your clients has been very helpful. I don't like missing videos because they've helped so much. I hope you don't stop putting the videos out there. I've tried all sorts of counseling and nothing has helped me the same way. It is amazing what you are doing. I was binge free for over four months, and then I slipped back. I learned, like you said, that if I still hope to lose weight, I will continue to suffer. I've had to focus a while to get that hope out of my head. Today I understand that. I am not my body. I am my soul inside. You have helped me so much to understand the root of the issue isn't my weight and size, but that I am wanting to feel valued and worth of love. I want to thank you.

Message from A 30-year-old Woman

Message: I came across your videos about a year ago. You were talking to a woman who had anorexia, and the advice you gave her really hit home with me. I started watching all of your videos and tried to apply what you were teaching in them. I especially learned how feeling bad about my body affects how I feel bad about food. Making this connection has been huge in helping see how those two things are connected. To end my eating issues, I need to come to terms with why I'm afraid of my body. Since finding your YouTube channel, my life and my view of myself has completely changed. I no longer worry about what my body looks like or what the scale says I weigh. I'm now very in-tune with my body, and I'm so happy not having to diet or worry about what I look like. This freedom from dieting and having to think about my body is amazing.

51-year-old-woman Who Suffered from Depression and Emotional Eating

Message: When I started watching Robin's videos about a year and a half ago, I was in the throws of dieting and had lost and gained 40 pound four times in a two-year period. Every time I stopped dieting, I started bingeing knowing I'd re-lose the weight again. I was watching a video when Robin had a client rate how catastrophic weight gain was compared to other physical problems. She had the client assess how hard it would be to lose her legs in an accident, and then had her rate how bad she felt about her weight. *This comparison made me realize how ridiculous the shame about my weight was and how unnecessary feeling bad about it was.* That's when I decided to work with Robin.

I had put my entire life on hold trying to fix my weight, focusing on trying to be thinner. I declined vacations, jobs, relationships, dating, and starting businesses because I condemned myself, blaming my larger body. Working with Robin for about a year, I really learned that if I want freedom in life, I can't hide and be afraid of it any more. And if I care about what other people think of my weight and body, I am giving them control over that freedom. It's been four years since, and I can't tell you how much everything this has changed in my life because of her wisdom and guidance. The freedom from feeling bad and from thinking about food all the time is beyond words. Because of our work together, my entire life has been set free.

I've started traveling, visiting over 20 cities, went back to school to take some classes, started dating, I am front and center in pictures now, have gone to the beach, and done so many things I thought had to wait until I was thinner. This is just incredible.

I've discovered that changing the way I feel about my body without needing my body to change, has made the greatest impact on my life than anything else I've ever done. I give Robin all the credit. She has an incredible amount of compassion for people, no matter how big they are and how much they struggle with body image and significant physical issues. She teaches people to honor themselves and their bodies and not to be ashamed any more, to start living their lives.

Message from A Woman in Her 40s

Message: I found your YouTube channel two years ago. You have helped me understand how I became so crazy while dieting obsessively. The concept of "thin supremacy" you talk about has completely changed the way I see the weight-loss industry. You operate from such an honest place and your sincerity is so clear in your videos. I can honestly say that I am done dieting, I love my body, and this has made a huge difference in my life. I am sure this will continue to make an impact long into my future.

Message from A Woman in Her Late 40s

Message: I have been binge watching your YouTube channel now for over a year. You've helped me realize that my binge-eating issues definitely stem from body image. Robin, what has helped me the most has been the forgiveness and grace you describe—and that's given me the room to listen to my body and learn that my body isn't the enemy. Since coming across your work, my bingeing has almost completely subsided. It didn't happen overnight, but *the more I love myself, and give myself grace, the easier it gets.*

22-year-old Woman Suffering from Anorexia

Message: I started feeling bad about my body at the age of four. I can distinctly remember a comment a boy in my class made: "I would marry her (pointing to a girl) but not her (pointing to me) because she's fat." I always felt different from my peers because of my weight, and assumed they didn't like me because of how I looked. I started dieting at the age of 10. My mother had just remarried a man who was a fitness fanatic, and I was constantly put on diets and encouraged to go to the gym. I was even spanked once because I refused to go. This is the time when bingeing became an issue. I would hide food and overeat when no one was watching because I would get in trouble if I was caught eating bad food.

Around the age of 13, I made friends with a girl that was like me, overweight and an underdog. The pressure to be thin kept growing so we decided it would be a good idea to lose weight together (bad idea). Things were good and "healthy" for a while before the inevitable dysfunction started to settle in. Long story short, I was emotionally eating while she was successfully starving herself. Of course, she was losing more weight than me, so I was determined to do what she was doing.

I started starving myself, going on juice cleanses, and over-exercising in hopes I would catch up to my friend's weight loss. I felt like she wasn't going to be my friend any more. But I never was able to successfully lose weight because the harder I tried, and the stricter the diets become, the more I binged. I gained around 70 pounds from age 13 to 16. I felt like a failure. My mind, youth, body, and friendships—all lost to body-image addiction.

I was 17 years old when I found your YouTube channel, Weight Loss Apocalypse. Watching your sessions with other people struggling like I was gave me a whole new perspective. At the beginning, was very difficult to let go of old beliefs about being thin and healthy that determined how I valued myself. It felt like death to deal with my greatest fears that family and friends wouldn't love me anymore. But as I began to love myself, *it was like the biggest cloud was lifted, and I could finally see what life was meant to be like.* Life isn't about having the thinnest tummy or space between your thighs. It's about experiencing things that actually feel good to me, like the smell of rain, feeling the breeze on a warm day, or the feeling of being around the people I love, and knowing they love me just as much—all things I never let myself enjoy because I was too busy chasing weight loss—and doing it for other people.

I'm 22 now, and I'm so grateful to have stumbled upon your videos when I was so young. It's been years since I stopped dieting, bingeing, and hiding myself from life. This way of being and having freedom has melted into every part of my life. Even though I struggled in such darkness as teenager, I would suffer the same way again if it means I can keep the peace of mind and confidence I have now going forward. Robin, thank you for *helping me learn to love myself.*

Woman in Her 60s Struggling with Body Image and Emotional Eating

Message: I met Robin after someone recommended that I read her book and watch her YouTube videos. After hearing her talk to other people struggling with emotional eating, I decided I wanted her help. The work we did together was unbelievable. Robin, thank you for helping me realize my relationship with food was connected to other aspects of my life. I learned so much about myself, and it has been life changing. It has been over five years since we've worked together, and I am still free from dieting, emotional eating, and worrying about my weight.

Message from A Woman in Her 20s

Message: I'm so grateful for these videos! Since discovering your work a few months ago, I have been experiencing a kind of peace and liberation that I never thought possible. For the first time since I was a little kid, I'm not preoccupied by negative feelings about my body, and I am more relaxed around food. My depression and anxiety symptoms are vanishing, and I must thank you because I feel like my authentic self is finally finding a voice.

A Woman in Her 30s Who Suffered from Anorexia

Message: Robin, after following you over five years, I owe you a THANK YOU. I've recently come into a full realization of who I really am. I am not my body! You and your videos were what sparked the flame years ago, and created a tear in the blinding veil of the ego. You gave me a glimpse of a whole world that existed outside the tiny box of anorexia that fear had confined me to. Now, I am experiencing complete freedom, and I'm feeling so much gratitude for the bits of true wisdom that you share in a world full of superficial advice. It took me five years to escape, but thanks for your sound wisdom and speaking from your own experience, I know that I will never go back to that tiny space of being. I don't know how to thank you enough. Thank you, thank you, thank you.

Message From a 38-year-old Woman

Message: I started gaining weight after a knee surgery in my mid 20s. Five years later, after feeling anxious and depressed, I started dieting. I tried being a vegetarian but as I became even more strict with food, I ended up with more emotional eating problems. That's when I found your YouTube channel…Weight Loss Apocalypse.

You have since has changed my life. I have been living by your words and with your philosophy for years now. I've stopped all dieting, lost my snobbish ways with food, and I don't binge any more. When I do emotionally eat, your YouTube sessions remind me to forgive and accept myself—and I feel this same compassion when I talk to other people also struggling to accept their weight. Having this grace has allowed me to treat myself and everyone else better.

Before I was letting other people influence my relationship with food, as well as make decisions for my life. Because of your experience, wisdom, and advice, I've taken responsibility and ownership of what's right for me, and it been an empowering process to direct my life from my own heart. I never would have thought this freedom and power would seep into other aspects of life.

This freedom has improved my emotional wellbeing and also my body. As my thoughts about food have become less rigid and more balanced and consistent, my weight stopped fluctuating wildly. I feel so much better. I no longer look to diets, weight loss, or others to confirm my worth as my goal now is to always be true to myself. I have your words to thank for that!

Woman in Her Late 30s—
Obsessive Exercise and Emotional Eating

Message: I've suffered with eating disorders since I was younger, and my mom took me to diet clinics when I was 11. I was a competitive gymnast as well as a ballerina. Since working with Robin, I can honestly say I will never diet or abuse my body with exercise again. She has helped change my life. I am professionally doing better, and I've had a complete career change. I am more confident, more relaxed, and am a happier person. I steer clear of abusive and codependent relationships that I used to gravitate toward. I love myself…and I would have never said this before. I'm at peace. I owe all of this to Robin. There is no one like her. It is incredibly rare to find someone who is as much of an expert and as intuitive as she is, and that combination is incredibly effective. I owe my life and my happiness that I now experience to Robin. She taught me about relationships, how important it is to love myself, and to take responsibility for my life and not leave it up to others.

Message From a 16-year-old Girl

Message: I started dieting when I was around age eleven, but I can remember feeling negative about my body as young as age nine. I have been a dancer (ballet, modern, jazz, tap, etc.) since I was three. It was always my dream and biggest passion in life. Then I began to greatly struggle with an eating disorder, which stripped me of everything I had previously loved.

Counting calories, restricting food groups, bingeing/purging, laxatives and exercise consumed my every thought. I was in a hospitalization program and saw various therapists. Yes, my physical health may have improved, but my mind was still in the same destructive place. It was not until I found Weight Loss Apocalypse on YouTube that I actually felt a sense of freedom from dieting.

I am now 16 years old, and I wouldn't call myself fully recovered, but I can confidently say that I am further from my eating disorder than I have ever been. With the help of these informative, educational and realistic videos, I learned that I needed to completely surrender myself to the body that I idealized in my head. This image is what kept me suffering. *I learned that I had to willingly accept myself where previously I would have deemed myself to be worthless.* I learned to let go of cultural standards which ultimately kept me a slave to the eating disorders. Once I separated myself entirely from the mere idea of thinness, I was able to implement the hunger and fullness scale. I can say that these videos have truly guided me to freedom from dieting. Now, thanks to your caring instructions and wisdom, instead of constantly feeling worried, I just feel relieved.

A 39-year-old Woman Suffering with Binge Eating Disorder

Message: I started to feel bad about my body around the age of 10 due to classmates making fun of my size— at the time my weight was totally normal. I started to sneak extra snacks and wanted "bad" food since I made food the enemy. As I got older, I tried numerous diets with my mother and friends and was "successful" in losing 100–150 pounds three separate times. I found myself bigger than ever and struggling to lose weight and desperately searched YouTube for help with my binge eating disorder. One of Robin's videos was suggested, so I took a chance and listened to it.

Through watching her videos and by working with her, I've learned that the human mind is designed to desire more food if you believe it's going away, like on a diet. As long as I continue to believe that I need to lose weight, I will continue to feel the need to diet, and I'll continue to overeat. I've learned that my body and instinct to eat isn't the actually the problem. The problem is believing the diet industry and society that suggests my body is bad and food is the enemy.

The hunger and fullness scale has given me freedom from bingeing and has helped me to not worry about when to eat or how much to eat. So much time has been wasted in the past worrying about food and which types of food are "good" or "bad" and what time of day I'm supposed to eat. None of that matters as much as trusting that my body can regulate itself. Freeing myself from dieting, and learning to eat based on the hunger and fullness scale, has been like pressing the reset button in order to learn how to eat the way my body was meant to.

A Woman in Her Late 20's

Message: My body was always a focus in my family. When I was six-years-old my parents thought I was too thin. Then at twelve-years-old, after my menstrual cycle began, my family thought I was too fat. In high school my grandmother told a doctor to put me on her diet medication, and that's when I became even more shameful about myself. I've had serious issues with dieting and food ever since.

I've had years of therapy, done mediation and reiki, and after finding your YouTube videos, I've found physical and spiritual freedom knowing I have unconditional worth. The hunger scale has taught me to listen to my body, which has freed me from dieting and worrying about food. Your words taught me to love myself and take responsibility for my life—and no longer allow others to do it for me. I now have time back to spend actively with my children, engaging and enjoying all the precious moments with them. I feel like I can fully enjoy life now.

> *"It's not my responsibility to be beautiful. I'm not alive for that purpose. My existence is not about how desirable you find me."*

– Warsan Shire, poet

Acknowledgments

I'd like to thank all the clients I've coached over the years who were willing to share their stories to the world on my YouTube channel. You are helping others by allowing them to witness your struggles and success in the process of recovery.

Next, I'd like to acknowledge and thank my copy development and line editor, Connie Anderson of Words and Deeds, Inc. Without her talents and the integrity of her work, I would have never finished this project, and it would've been far more difficult to read. Connie has been an imperative partner in capturing for the reader what I am trying to communicate. She is incredibly gifted and has been an essential influence to this body of work. Many people had told me that I'm a good writer—but my response is to let them know I have an incredible editor.

A special thank you to Denise Watson and Dr. Ed Hagen from Vivify Integrative Health in Hudson, Wisconsin. You gave me the opportunity to teach your patients, one by one, for years. Repeating the same explanation over and over, hundreds of times, was an invaluable part of refining how I teach the Mind:Body Method to participants. This work with you has been precious.

Thank you to my professors at Boise State University. Without such rigorous educational standards, I couldn't have understood the research that provided the basis for the content discussed in this book. To the Kinesiology department: Thank you for having such passion for the health of the human mind and body.

My hard-working and humble parents—for being the ultimate examples of perseverance and integrity. To sister Katie for your incredible artistic mind, and for the book title and cover design. To her and all my other siblings—Steve, Laura, Daniel, Jennalee, Debbie, Becky, Melissa, Cliff, Mike, Big Jeff, Little Jeff, and Jean—for helping develop my "character."

References

(1.) Walter B. Cannon (1927). *Bodily Changes in Pain, Hunger, Fear, and Rage: An Account of Recent Researches into the Function of Emotional Excitement.* Harvard University.

(2.) Joseph E LeDoux Ph.D. (2015) FEAR: The Amygdala Is NOT the Brain's Fear Center, Separating findings from conclusions. *Psychology Today.*
https://www.psychologytoday.com/us/blog/i-got-mind-tell-you/201508/the-amygdala-is-not-the-brains-fear-center

(3.) Satter, Ellyn. (2007). Eating competence: definition and evidence for the Satter Eating Competence model. *Journal of Nutrition Education and Behavior.* Sep-Oct; 39(5): S142-53 doi:10.1016/j.jneb.2007.01.006

(4.) Engeln-Maddox, R. (2005). Cognitive responses to idealized media images of women: The relationship of social comparison and critical processing to body image disturbance in college women. *Journal of Social and Clinical Psychology.* 24(8),
1114-1138. https://doi.org/10.1521/jscp.2005.24.8.1114

(5.) Dittmar, Helga (2007). The Costs of Consumer Culture and the "Cage Within": The Impact of the Material "Good Life" and "Body Perfect" Ideals on Individuals" *Identity and Well-*

Being, Psychological Inquiry. 18(1), 23-31, DOI: 10.1080/10478400701389045

(6.) Kristin Neff, Ph D. (2015). *Self-Compassion: The Proven Power of Being Kind to Yourself.* William Morrow Paperbacks

(7.) Roberts T-A, Gettman JY. (2004). Mere exposure: Gender differences in the negative effects of priming a state of self-objectification. *Sex Roles.* Vol51:17–27. doi: 10.1023/B:SERS.0000032306.20462.22

(8.) Schaefer LM, Thompson JK. (2018). Self-objectification and disordered eating: A meta-analysis. *International Journal of Eating Disorders.* Jun:51(6):483-502. doi: 10.1002/eat.22854

(9.) Kathryn H. Gordon, Joseph J. Dombeck. (2010) The associations between two facets of narcissism and eating disorder symptoms. *Eating Behaviors.* Vol 11(4): 288-292. doi: 10.1016/j.eatbeh.2010.08.004

(10.) Alan Rappoport, Ph D. (2005). Co-Narcissism: How We Accommodate to Narcissistic Parents. *San Francisco Psychotherapy Research Group.* http://alanrappoport.com/pdf/Co-Narcissism%20Article.pdf

(11.) Elise Carrotte, Joel Anderson. (2018). Risk factor or protective feature? The roles of grandiose and hypersensitive narcissism in explaining the relationship between self-objectification and body image concerns. *Sex Roles.* 10.1007/s11199-018-0948-y.

(12.) Sivanathan, D., Bizumic, B., Rieger, E. et al. (2019). Vulnerable narcissism as a mediator of the relationship between perceived parental invalidation and eating disorder pathology. *Eating and Weight Disorders.* Vol 24: 1071–1077. https://doi.org/10.1007/s40519-019-00647-2

(13.) Crystal D. Oberle, Razieh O. Samaghabadi, Elizabeth M. Hughes. (2017). Orthorexia nervosa: Assessment and correlates with gender, BMI, and personality. *Appetite.* Vol 108: 303-310. https://doi.org/10.1016/j.appet.2016.10.021

(14.) Antonios Dakanalis, Massimo Clerici, Guiseppe Carra. (2015). Narcissistic Vulnerability and Grandiosity as Mediators Between Insecure Attachment and Future Eating Disordered Behaviors: A Prospective Analysis of Over 2,000 Freshman. *Journal of Clinical Psychology.* Vol 72(3): 279-292. doi:10.1002/jclp.22237

(15.) Waller G; Sines J; Meyer C; Foster E; Skelton A. (2007) Narcissism and narcissistic defenses in the eating disorders. *International Journal of Eating Disorders.* Vol 40(2):143-8 DOI:10.1002/eat.20345

(16.) Sines, Jennie & Waller, Glenn & Meyer, Caroline & Wigley, Laura. (2008). Core beliefs and narcissistic characteristics among eating-disordered and non-clinical women. *Psychology and Psychotherapy.* Vol 81: 121-129. Doi:10.1348/147608307X267496

(17.) Jessica Maples, Brittany Collins, Joshua D. Miller, Sarah Fischer, Alana Seibert. (2011). Differences between grandiose and vulnerable narcissism and bulimic symptoms in young women. *Eating Behaviors.* Vol 12 (1): 83-85. https://doi.org/10.1016/j.eatbeh.2010.10.001

(18.) Waller, Glenn & Sines, Jennie & Meyer, Caroline & Mountford, Victoria. (2008). Body checking in the eating disorders: Association with narcissistic characteristics. Eating Behaviors. Vol 9: 163-9. Doi:10.1016/j.eatbeh.2007.07.004

(19.) Steven Bratman, MD, MPH. (2017). What is Orthorexia? http://www.orthorexia.com/

(20.) Michael Adorjan, Tony Christensen, Benjamin Kelly, Dorothy Pawluch. (2012). Stockholm Syndrome as Vernacular Resource. *The Sociological Quarterly*. Vol 53(3): 454-474. Doi: 10.1111/j.1533-8525.2012.01241.x

(21.) Celia Jameson. (2010). The "Short Step" from Love to Hypnosis: a Reconsideration of the Stockholm Syndrome. *Journal for Cultural Research*. Vol 14(4): 337-355. Doi: 10.1080/14797581003765309

(22.) Judith Lewis Herman. (1992). Complex PTSD: A syndrome in survivors of prolonged and repeated trauma. *Journal of Traumatic Stress*. Vol 5(3): 377-391.

(23.) Angela Ebert, Murray J. Dyck. (2004). The experience of mental death: the core feature of complex posttraumatic stress disorder. *Clinical Psychology Review*. Vol 24: 617-635. Doi:10.1016/j.cpr.2004.06.002

(24.) Ying-Hsien Chao, Chao-Chin Yang, Wen-Bin Chiou. (2012) Food as ego-protective remedy for people experiencing shame. Experimental evidence for a new perspective on weight-related shame. *Appetite*. 59(2): 570-575. https://doi.org/10.1016/j.appet.2012.07.007

(25.) James Gilligan. (2003). Shame, guilt, and violence. *Social Research: An International Quarterly.* Vol 70 (4):1149-1180

(26.) Tangney, J. P., Miller, R. S., Flicker, L., & Barlow, D. H. (1996). Are shame, guilt, and embarrassment distinct emotions? *Journal of Personality and Social Psychology.* 70(6): 1256–1269. https://doi.org/10.1037/0022-3514.70.6.1256

(27.) M. Macht and G. Simons. (2000). Emotions and Eating in Everyday Life. *Appetite.* 35(1): 65-71. doi:10.1006/appe.2000.0325

(28.) Hawkins, David.R. (2018) Map of Consciousness. *Book of Slides (The Complete Collection) Presented at the 2002-2011 Lectures with Clarifications.* Pages: 12,104-107

After publishing *Weight-Loss Apocalypse* in 2011, author Robin Phipps Woodall started a YouTube Channel to share her coaching sessions that helped people who struggled to stop emotional eating. As Woodall met with each of her coaching clients, she found that her significant experience with an eating disorder, as well as her miraculous recovery, kept coming up in their discussions. For thousands of followers, Woodall's story was only understood through bits and pieces discussed in these YouTube videos.

In this book, Woodall tells how in the matter of a couple of years she went from being a cheerful college student to suffering with suicidal depression and a relentless eating disorder. While in a deep state of contemplation as she emotionally prepared to end her life, Woodall miraculously recovered. Not only did she experience an instantaneous removal from every negative aspect of the disorder and depression, but she also came out of it having a total shift in the way she perceived and lived life.

After over 20 years of being totally recovered, Robin Woodall is excited to tell you her story: *My Weight-Loss Apocalypse.*

After 8 years, author Robin Phipps Woodall has updated *Weight-Loss Apocalypse*, adding 52 pages of new mind-opening content. In the second edition, along with the important discussions of Dr. Simeons' hCG protocol, the need for further scientific investigation, and the hunger and fullness scale, Robin examines further the impact dieting has on emotional eating.

She explains: Until the influence that dieting has on over-eating or emotional eating is exposed as problematic, the demand for excessive amounts of food will continue, and weight gain will always be viewed as the problem. This additional discussion is instrumental in preparing the reader for the next book in the series: *Weight-Loss Apocalypse, Book 2*, which complements this book by addressing how body image negatively impacts how people approach Dr. Simeons' protocol.

For this reason, Robin is excited to present this updated second edition as *Weight-Loss Apocalypse, Book 1*.

"Robin has done it again. Whether you're new to the hCG protocol, or you've done the protocol more times than you'd like to admit this groundbreaking book is for you."

– Becky Sumsion, RDN, CD, Life Coach, Author

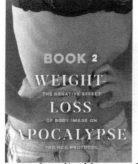

After over a decade of continued observation, author Robin Phipps Woodall is excited to share what she's discovered regarding the emotional impact of Dr. Simeons' hCG protocol. In *Weight-Loss Apocalypse– Book 2*, Robin examines the affect that negative body image has on a person's impulse to diet—and how repeated cyclical bouts of the hCG protocol done for this reason can be emotionally and physically harmful. Disarming beliefs that impel people to feel bad about their body is an essential step when approaching the hCG protocol, not as a diet, but as a serious medical treatment.

In this book, Robin describes the psychological risks of the very low-calorie protocol as well as the importance of an emotional evaluation, alongside a physical evaluation, in determining whether a person is an appropriate candidate for the hCG protocol.

For thousands of years, cultures have pushed physical ideas and concepts of the body as a way for people to achieve superiority and success. Like foot binding to make feet smaller, or the use of corsets to minimize waist size, many of these body images result in painful disability and disfigurement. Today the "superior" body being pushed comes from ideas of health and attractiveness as seen through images of ultra-lean thinness. Author Robin Phipps Woodall calls this "the culture of thin supremacy."

In *Thin Supremacy*, Woodall connects the individual's drive to achieve superior body images to human survival instincts, compelling people to fit in as a way to be viewed as worthy of love and inclusion. Unfortunately, as images of worth based on thinness have become more and more unrealistic, sadly this is on the rise: people suffering from emotional issues stemming from shame about their body. Woodall confronts the culture of thin supremacy—and encourages the reader to question their beliefs about body image.

In this book, author Robin Phipps Woodall builds on the significant discussion of body image from her first book, *Thin Supremacy*. Here she expands further to explore the overwhelming—and sometimes traumatic or even tragic—impact that negative body image has on dieting and emotional eating.

From the viewpoint of evolutionary psychology, in *Diet Supremacy*, Woodall illustrates how fears of social stigma, based on body fat, trigger primitive survival mechanisms that motivate people to seek safety and control through forms of "diet supremacy." The toxic bond between negative body image and dieting while surrounded by abundance of food, promotes the angst and strain responsible for increasing one's feeling of deprivation. The result is an increase in cravings, perceived hunger, and the impulsive drive to eat excessively. This is an important topic every weight-loss business, dieter, emotional eater, and eating disorder specialist needs to know about, understand, and especially discuss with those affected.

In *Body Supremacy*, author Robin Phipps Woodall expands on her first book, *Thin Supremacy*, and her second book, *Diet Supremacy*, to describe how these narcissistic belief systems combine to form the foundation for an eating disorder to develop. From the perspective of her own amazing recovery, Woodall presents a discussion about eating disorders as a psychological syndrome stemming from mechanisms of survival. A person suffering with an eating disorder is fighting to survive, even though her defense mechanisms are in fact killing her.

This book would interest a reader who wants to study and understand a different point of view for why people hold themselves hostage inside the darkness of an eating disorder. If you are studying eating disorders, work with people who suffer inside the darkness of an eating disorder, or are suffering yourself, this most-informative book was written for you.

In *Surrendering Your Survival,* author Robin Phipps Woodall describes the perspective of living your life while coming out of the self-centered nature of survival mode that was previously controlled by "thin and diet" supremacy belief systems. When a person rejects those belief systems to instead accept herself unconditionally, survival mechanisms calm down, and her mind shifts open. As people are liberated from narcissistic body images and diet supremacy, they are left to question how they should eat moving forward.

For this reason, Woodall describes in *Surrendering Your Survival* the science of hunger and satiety, as well as how important these physical senses are when relearning how to eat without fear or shame. The goal is to renew your relationship with your body and food in such a way that they are not the focus of your life as you move forward. This leads to the glorious and life-saving freedom people experience when they are recovered.

FOR MORE INFORMATION

Website: *https://weightlossapocalypse.com*

Email: *info@mindbodyhcg.com*

YouTube: *https://youtube.com/user/weightlossapocalypse*

Instagram: *@WeightLossApocalypse*

Twitter: *@MindBodyMethod*

Facebook: *Weight-Loss Apocalypse*

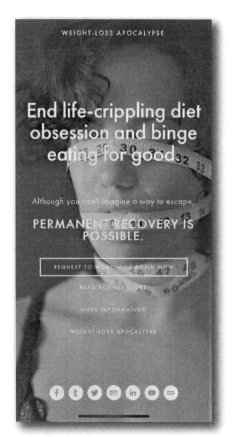

Made in the USA
Columbia, SC
01 July 2021

41278779R00157